FACING AIDS

FACING AIDS

The Challenge,
the Churches' Response

*A WCC **Study** Document*

WCC Publications, Geneva

Second printing 2000
Third printing 2001

Cover design: Edwin Hassink

Cover photo: WCC/Peter Williams

ISBN 2-8254-1213-9

© 1997 WCC Publications, World Council of Churches,
150 route de Ferney, 1211 Geneva 2, Switzerland
Website: http://www.wcc-coe.org

Printed in Switzerland

Table of Contents

Foreword

In the foreword to the first edition of this study document Ana Langerak spoke of the complexities of "the impact of HIV/AIDS on the everyday life of families, churches, communities and peoples". Langerak went on to emphasize the need to consider the pandemic in the widest and deepest sense if we were to fathom the implications of AIDS in ethical, social, economic and political life. Three years later the challenge for the churches is even greater.

Since the first printing of this book, there has been a tremendous change in the magnitude of the pandemic. In 1997 the World Health Organization estimated the number of infected persons at 25 million (mid-1996 figures). The rate of increase was put at 7000 per day, including 1400 babies. Assuming the rate has been reasonably constant, then the estimate for today is approximately 36 million worldwide. Similarly, the political economy of HIV/AIDS has shifted significantly. The politics of HIV/AIDS is becoming increasingly complex. The relationship between AIDS and poverty, AIDS and structural violence, and even the question of the origins of AIDS are among the controversial issues in the current HIV/AIDS discourse.

The importance of a reprint of this study document cannot therefore be overemphasized. Alongside other WCC publications on the subject, it has been a valuable companion to churches and social organizations seeking to deepen and broaden their understanding of and work on HIV/AIDS. *The Church and AIDS in Africa* cites the WCC publications on HIV/AIDS among the most valued resource materials widely used in Africa.

By having clear foci on three areas that help the ecumenical movement and the churches to shape their response to HIV/AIDS, this study has carved a niche in the concomitant discourse. While each of the three areas (theology and ethics, pastoral care and the church as a healing community, and justice and human rights) has a distinct paradigm, they are integrally connected. Seen from the integral perspective they challenge us to go even deeper in analyzing and asking hard questions around several dimensions; relational, structural and political.

The disease of AIDS is a serious invitation for us to reflect on human relations at communal and global levels. Part of the problem is the commodification of human relations. Globalization greatly exacerbates this problem by promoting a consumer mentality whereby sexuality, itself reduced to a commodity, can no longer be separated from a surplus. In promoting prevention measures it is imperative to have the wider picture – to restore to sexuality its integrity. The tendency to treat sexuality as a commodity leads to emphasis on technical advice, i.e. to increase the use of condoms. The moral admonition to remain faithful has its limitations because its emphasis is more on the individual rather than the community.

A sufficient and effective control of AIDS will depend more on the quality of human relations and of our institutions. Similarly, a new culture of sexuality is needed whereby sexual encounter has to be viewed in its communal dimension instead of stressing one-dimensional and individual-oriented self-realization as the highest value. Benezet Bujo could not have put it more correctly when he argued: "Although the problem of AIDS is too often linked to sexuality alone, it must be put forward explicitly that our materialistic desires also let many people fall victims of this disease. Illicit trading in drugs and the recycling of 'dirty' money must be mentioned here. These two are basic vices which deprive the human person of dignity in a brutal manner. Again, these vices do not affect only individuals, but they affect especially those institutions which support such crimes in the name of profit."

Structural and social violence must be included in any serious discourse on HIV/AIDS. What are the relationships between poverty, gender, disease and AIDS? The mutually re-enforcing effects of poverty and AIDS are becoming more evident. The advent of structural adjustment programmes (SAPs) precipitated an economic crisis which accelerated the spread of HIV/AIDS. In turn the ravages of AIDS plunge the afflicted areas deeper into economic crisis, creating a vicious cycle. In their wake, moreover, SAP policies reversed the trend of achievements in health of the last three decades.

In several affected areas life expectancy has been greatly reduced and the mortality rate has gone up. Poverty and gender inequality make women particularly vulnerable to AIDS. By undermining the viability of rural economies, SAP policies and oppressive governance have put women at an even greater risk of HIV infection.

The initial response to AIDS was considerably influenced by the prevailing political thinking. To a very large extent public health action is a function of political considerations which take place in the context of contested meanings and unequal power.

When it comes to resource allocation the rural areas usually get a raw deal. The urban elite who dominate political power considered HIV/AIDS as an "urban disease" and for a long time health budgetary allocations were skewed in favour of the urban areas. That situation was not helped by the health plans of the powerful development agencies. The latter also concentrated their work in urban centres. It was a long time before the key players recognized AIDS as a development issue. In sub-Saharan Africa, where the majority of populations reside in the rural areas, it is imperative that adequate health resources are allocated to help the rural folk face up to the daunting challenge of HIV/AIDS in their midst.

The newly formed Ecumenical Advocacy Alliance (EAA) chose HIV/AIDS alongside with economic justice as the two most pressing issues around which to do global advocacy. In choosing HIV/AIDS, EAA acknowledged the pandemic to be "one of the greatest health challenges facing the world at the moment. It is also, arguably, the gravest challenge to prospects of social and economic development and global security."

By reprinting this study document the WCC reaffirms that a response to the challenges of HIV/AIDS is a top priority on the ecumenical agenda. We commend the book not only to churches and ecumenical organizations but to the wider community because, in a sense, the whole of humanity today is "living with HIV/AIDS".

Sam Kobia
Director
WCC Cluster on Issues and Themes

CHAPTER 1

Why This Study Was Prepared

The global epidemic — or "pandemic" — of the Human Immunodeficiency Virus (HIV) and the consequent Acquired Immunodeficiency Syndrome (AIDS) has evoked responses from many national governments, United Nations bodies and non-governmental organizations. There are many reasons for the churches to respond to this challenge and to join hands with the worldwide effort to provide care and support, to reduce vulnerability to HIV and to alleviate the impact of the pandemic.

For many of us HIV/AIDS has acted as a spotlight, exposing and revealing many iniquitous conditions in our personal and community lives which until now we have not been willing to confront. The pandemic reveals the tragic consequences of personal actions which directly harm others, and of negligence which opens persons to additional risk. It exposes any silence and indifference of the churches, challenging them to be better informed, more active and more faithful witnesses to the gospel of reconciliation in their own lives and in their communities.

Increasing numbers of people worldwide are falling sick, suffering physically, emotionally and spiritually — many in abandonment and desolation. Men, women, young people and children are dying; families and communities are severely affected socially and economically, particularly in less affluent countries. The effects of HIV/AIDS are impoverishing people, breaking their hearts, violating their human rights and wreaking havoc on their bodies and spirits.

Jesus Christ demonstrated God's love to all human beings, coming to be present in the midst of human struggle. If the churches are to fulfill their mission, they must recognize that HIV/AIDS brings the lives of many people into crisis and that it is a crisis which churches must face. The very relevance of the churches will be determined by their response. The crisis also challenges the churches to re-examine the human conditions which in fact promote the pandemic and to sharpen their awareness of people's inhumanity to one other, of broken relationships and unjust structures, and of their own complacency and complicity. HIV/AIDS is a sign of the times, calling us to see and to understand.

It was for these reasons that the central committee of the World Council of Churches, meeting in Johannesburg, South Africa, in 1994, mandated the formation of a consultative group to conduct a study on HIV/AIDS that would help the ecumenical movement to shape its response in the three areas of theology and ethics, pastoral care and the church as healing community, and justice and human rights. The study should challenge the churches to be more honest, more faithful and better informed — and to become communities which are safe places for people living with HIV/AIDS.

This *study document* is the result of that process. It sets the work done by sub-groups in each of the three areas within the overall framework of the global challenges posed by AIDS, and the urgent need for a faithful and creative response from the churches. The study document was received by the committee on WCC Programme Unit II (Churches in Mission: Health, Education, Witness) during the meeting of the central committee in September 1996. The full central committee welcomed the document and commended it to the churches for reflection and appropriate action.

The WCC central committee also *officially adopted* — significantly, with no dissenting votes — a substantial concise *statement* on "The Impact of HIV/AIDS and the Churches' Response". This text, which distills and focuses the issues explored in the longer study document, is also included in this volume (see Appendix I, p.96).

The different sections of this report show some variations in style, reflecting the contributions of diverse group members and, in some cases, the characteristic tone and vocabulary of particular subject areas. The report also includes a number of texts printed within boxes. This material is of several different types, including statements by church bodies; testimonies, stories and personal narratives; case study material from local churches; and excerpts from reports of scientific studies and from United Nations study programmes. These are included to enrich and enliven the report, and to bring in a wider range of voices and expertise than is sometimes heard in the discussion within the churches about the HIV/AIDS pandemic.

The study process out of which these chapters have grown has itself been an ecumenical journey. People with experience and expertise in various fields related to HIV/AIDS, coming from all continents and many confessions, and including some persons living with HIV/AIDS, came together to be a part of this journey.

The knowledge and opinions held by members of the consultative group were as diverse as their geographical and confessional backgrounds. The first task therefore was to listen to and to learn from each other. And this process was not always easy. It required a spirit of humility. There was tension between widely differing views, and long deliberation over sensitive issues. In the course of the study many firmly held convictions were rethought in the light of new information and the experience of others.

At various stages of this ecumenical journey members of the consultative group were exposed to the realities of communities and individuals living with HIV/AIDS and working in AIDS-related projects. During these exposure visits — which took place in South Africa, the USA and India — preliminary findings from the study were shared with local community members, and their comments invited. This was done to avoid producing an overly "academic" report far removed from the struggles, sufferings and celebrations of people's real lives. Many people, therefore, who were not officially part of the consultative group have contributed to the report and deserve credit for what has been achieved.

A most remarkable experience for those on this journey was the high degree of unity and common vision, despite differences and seemingly irreconcilable positions. All made a sincere attempt to comprehend the background and honest intentions of others, even if differing conclusions were reached in some areas. In this way, the study process was a true experience of ecumenical learning. There was also a sense among members of the group that God's Spirit was enabling them to accept each other as sisters and brothers working together for the common good. The rich worship life in all meetings and consultations was a constant source of inspiration and support. It brought discussions and resolutions into the presence of the living God who is there as we gather to pray, sing, learn, mourn and celebrate life.

This report, therefore, is written with the firm conviction that we do not "possess" the truth but are constantly to search for God's will in a changing world. In the worldwide struggle to find answers to the challenge of HIV/AIDS there are almost every day new discoveries, new information, new responses and new reports on how communities are affected by this pandemic. No report issued at any particular point in time will provide the final answers to this challenge; it can only be part of a continuing process.

It must also be remembered that issues related to HIV/AIDS are extremely complex. While HIV is a virus and AIDS the medical consequence of viral infection, the related issues are far from being simply medical or clinical concerns. They affect, and are affected by, cultural norms and practices, socio-economic conditions, development and gender issues, sexuality and many other factors.

This report approaches the challenge of HIV/AIDS from different perspectives: science, the socio-economic context, theology, ethics, human rights, the churches as healing communities, pastoral care and education. All these aspects are interlinked, and cannot be completely separated from one another. Specific aspects, however, are identifiable within the report for readers who wish to refer to issues of particular interest to them.

Even though this report is part of an ongoing process, and the issues are extremely complex, readers should not be discouraged. They should not succumb to pessimistic resignation or puzzled inactivity. Individuals, communities and countries are in urgent need because of the continued spread of the pandemic. The lives and well-being of countless people rely on decisions and actions which are required today. All institutions, not least the churches and their congregations, bear a great responsibility in responding to this challenge, and must help all people and their communities to the best of their knowledge and ability.

From the beginning of the pandemic some Christians, churches and church-related institutions have been active in education and prevention programmes, and in caring for people living with HIV/AIDS. The consultative group was privileged to have worked with several of these during the study. But it is the judgment of the group that by and large the response of the churches has been inadequate and has, in some cases, even made the problem worse. As the WCC executive committee noted in 1987, "through their silence, many churches share responsibility for the fear that has swept our world more quickly than the virus itself". [1] Sometimes churches have hampered the spread of accurate information, or created barriers to open discussion and understanding. Sometimes they have reinforced racist attitudes by neglecting issues of HIV/AIDS because it occurs predominantly among certain ethnic or racial groups, who may be unjustly stigmatized as the most likely carriers of the infection.

The situation calls for a fresh resolve by the churches to address the challenge of HIV/AIDS directly. This report seeks to enable churches, their members and leaders to act courageously and to make well-informed decisions in the light of the information currently available. Initiatives adapted to local situations must be taken in response to the real needs of individuals and communities affected by HIV/AIDS. But action requires first awareness-building and, not least, openness to acknowledging and discussing sensitive issues related to this pandemic.

Finally, it is the churches themselves which are affected by HIV/AIDS, and their credibility depends on the way in which they respond. They are confronted with people, members of the body of Christ, who not only seek support and solidarity, but who ask: Do you want to be my brother and sister?

NOTE

[1] Quoted in the *Minutes* of the 38th meeting of the WCC central committee, Geneva, WCC, 1987, Appendix VI, "AIDS and the Church as a Healing Community", p.135.

CHAPTER 2

Facing HIV/AIDS

The scientific facts: an introduction

Diseases emerge or re-emerge in different parts of the world from time to time. Occasionally a disease is "discovered" which may in fact have been prevalent for some time. Such phenomena have in general been limited geographically to certain ecological niches where conditions were conducive for the "new", emerging or re-emerging disease. AIDS, by contrast, is truly a *new* disease. Its ecological niche seems to cover the whole world. In its wake it has brought many surprises. It has shocked us into reflection.

AIDS stands for

Acquired (not genetically determined)

Immunodeficiency (severe depletion of immune system cells, that is, the cells which defend the body from other, even trivial, infections)

Syndrome (an illness which presents itself in various forms)

The origins of AIDS are unknown; however, it was first recognized in the USA during 1981. Initially it was reported among gay men, and was causing death at an early age. These two aspects were publicized sensationally by the mass media worldwide, etching the notion "AIDS = gay plague" on the minds of people everywhere. The aversion and fear which this notion promoted have remained, despite clear evidence to the contrary. After gay men the next most commonly stereotyped group to be affected was intravenous drug-users, thus further reinforcing negative attitudes.

Such prejudices are still alive today, although more and more groups are being affected. AIDS increasingly strikes women, children, heterosexuals, and those who have not been sexually active. It strikes not just persons "out there", but members of local communities, familiar neighbours and even family members. Sadly, many Christians and some churches have shared in the promotion of negative, judgmental and condemnatory attitudes.

By 1982, AIDS had been detected in some African countries (in fact, it was found to have been responsible for high fatality rates there since the 1970s). It was affecting heterosexuals, both men and women, who were neither homosexual nor injecting drug-users. Thus AIDS was known to be transmitted by sexual contact — regardless of gender — and by blood (for example, through needle-sharing or blood transfusions). It also became clear that sexual transmission was related to having many sexual partners. This new connection with sexual promiscuity entrenched self-righteous, negative judgments about people living with HIV/AIDS.

In 1983-84 the virus causing the immunodeficiency was identified. Although previously known by other names, it is now called HIV (Human Immunodeficiency Virus). It has continued to spread without detection among many people in new places. By the time this report was completed, HIV infection had reached nearly all countries of the world; and families everywhere are beginning to be affected by AIDS. It has thus become a pandemic. For people in towns, villages and parishes, it is causing local epidemics. The infection and disease, at first an epidemic (referring to a disease with a rapid and increasing rate of spread), are becoming *endemic*, that is, entrenched and spreading steadily. Epidemics go away; endemic diseases remain.

The chain of transmission of HIV/AIDS is not at all limited to persons having sexual contact with multiple partners.

• A spouse living in a faithful monogamous sexual relationship may become infected if his or her partner was infected earlier, either through sexual contact or needle-sharing drug use.

• HIV has spread and continues to spread in health-care settings due to unscreened blood transfusions and the reuse of needles and syringes without adequate cleaning and sterilization.

• Infants born to HIV-infected women are also at risk of becoming infected with HIV. This is called "vertical" transmission. Between 15 and 40 percent of infants born to HIV-infected mothers develop HIV infection through vertical transmission.

HIV infection is a silent phenomenon which can be diagnosed only by blood tests. By itself it is not a disease. However, infected persons remain internally virus-infected for life, and they are therefore infectious to others through blood or other body-fluids contact. As a result of prolonged HIV infection the immune system weakens, and as a result of this immune deficiency the person becomes susceptible to secondary diseases. This phase, marked by opportunistic infections, cancers or other debilitating conditions, is generally called HIV-disease or AIDS.

In spite of intensive biomedical research no cure has been found for the immune deficiency caused by HIV infection. Although several anti-viral drugs have been developed, the virus has developed resistance against all of them. This is partly due to the ability of the virus to mutate and change through a process of adaptation. As a result of such changes the virus has differentiated into subtypes in different geographical regions. Continuing attempts to develop an effective vaccine against HIV infection have also been unsuccessful so far; and it is generally believed that a single vaccine may not be effective against all subtypes. In short, a biomedical cure or vaccine for HIV/AIDS remains an elusive goal.

At the individual level, HIV infection is potentially preventable if one avoids the risk factors which facilitate the transmission of infection. In sexual activity, partners exchange sexual secretions and, along with them, microbes that are normally present in abundance on the genital mucosal surfaces. These are called the normal microbial flora; we acquire them normally from our environment during the physiological processes of growth and development. Having sex with a single partner in mutual monogamy ensures that both partners have only the normal flora.

Pathogenic microbes that cause diseases such as syphilis, gonorrhoea, genital herpes, chancroid and so on can be acquired only from another infected person through sexual contact. These are known as sexually transmitted diseases (STDs). Because HIV is sexually transmitted, AIDS is also an STD. Unlike most sexually transmitted diseases, HIV/AIDS does not cause disease of the local genital mucosa and skin. However, the presence of an STD, particularly one with an ulcerative lesion, facilitates the transmission of HIV between sexual partners if one of them has the infection. Since HIV is transmitted less readily and less often in the absence of any local lesion, the early detection, diagnosis and correct treatment of all other

STDs will reduce the risk of HIV transmission, even when one of the partners is infected with HIV.

The chance of sexual transmission of any pathogen, including HIV, is minimal or none if an effective barrier is used to prevent physical contact between the mucosal surfaces of the sex partners. The barrier also prevents the exchange of genital secretions. This is the principle behind the use of condoms to prevent HIV transmission. The condom is to be worn by the male partner; a condom to be worn by the female partner has also been designed and field-tested.

The magnitude of the problem

When AIDS emerged two decades ago, few people could predict how the epidemic would evolve. We know now from experience that AIDS can devastate whole regions, wipe out decades of national development, widen the gulf between rich and poor nations, and push already stigmatized groups closer to the margins of society. Experience also shows that the right approaches, applied quickly enough and with courage and resolve, can and do result in lower HIV infection rates and less suffering for those affected by the epidemic.

The Joint United Nations Programme on HIV/AIDS (UNAIDS) and the World Health Organization (WHO) estimates that the number of people living with HIV or AIDS by the end of the year 2000 stood at 36.1 million.[1] Already 21.8 million people around the world have died of AIDS, 4.3 million of them children. The most recent estimates show that, in the year 2000 alone, 5.3 million people were newly infected with HIV. This pandemic has also orphaned 13.2 million children.

Of the 36.1 million people with HIV/AIDS, 25.3 million (70 percent) live in sub-Saharan Africa. In sixteen countries in this region over 10 percent of the people are infected with HIV, and in six of them 20 percent are infected. Successful prevention programmes in a handful of African countries, notably Uganda, have reduced national infection rates and show the way ahead for other nations.

The region of South and Southeast Asia is estimated to have 5.8 million adults and children living with HIV or AIDS. In East Asia, most of its huge adult population has an HIV prevalence rate of 0.07

percent, as compared with 0.56 percent in South and Southeast Asia. The epidemic in East Asia has ample room for growth as there is a steep rise in the incidence of sexually transmitted diseases in the region.

In Latin America and the Caribbean 1.8 million people live with HIV/AIDS. The epidemic in this region is a complex mosaic of transmission patterns in which HIV continues to spread through homosexual transmission.

In Eastern Europe and Central Asia the estimated number of adults and children living with HIV or AIDS at the end of 1999 was 420,000. Just one year later, a conservative estimate put the figure at 700,000. Most of the quarter million adults who became infected were men, the majority of them injecting-drug users.

There is compelling evidence[2] to show that the trend in HIV infection will have a profound impact on future rates of infant, child and maternal mortality, life expectancy and economic growth. These unprecedented impacts at the macro-level are matched by the intense burden of suffering among individuals and households. Caring for those who are infected remains an enormous national and international challenge. Caring for the orphans the epidemic has left behind compounds this task. Protection of another generation of young people from premature illness and death is a responsibility of the highest order.

Prevention of HIV transmission

The magnitude of the problem and the current speed of expansion of the HIV pandemic make prevention a primary concern.

Since the beginning of the pandemic, knowledge about the best methods of preventing the transmission of HIV has increased tremendously. The learning process has been difficult and painful. Many approaches have been unhelpful or even damaging, and the implementation of effective methods has often been slow, or has suffered from insufficient funding. These obstacles have cost the lives of countless people. After careful evaluation of the successes and failures of many approaches and programmes, a number of effective interventions are now available. These include the following.

1. Information, education, communication

The prevention of HIV transmission requires first and foremost that people are properly informed about how the virus can — and cannot — be transmitted from one person to another. Understanding these facts should enable people to make responsible choices that will prevent this transmission. But information alone is not enough to determine human behaviour, which is related to deep emotions, to socio-economic conditions and to cultural and traditional norms and values. And in many situations freedom of choice is absent, so that persons are prevented from acting wisely.

Participatory approaches are required in which education is linked to experience. Key elements to be borne in mind in planning information, education, communication programmes are:

- the educational messages must be clear and easy to comprehend, using appropriate media targeted specifically on the groups to be educated;
- the most effective educators are people directly affected by HIV/AIDS;
- the community must be involved in identifying the cultural and social practices which increase or decrease the risk of HIV transmission, and in formulating education programmes appropriate for its situation;
- peer groups — persons from the same age range who are acquainted with the social and cultural environment of the target groups — are much more effective in education than people coming from "outside".

Generally speaking, messages using fear and negative images of AIDS have not been effective in producing or sustaining changes of behaviour.

2. Reduction of sexual transmission

Sexual transmission of HIV can be prevented by avoiding sexual behaviour which leads to an increased exposure to HIV. The safest options are sexual abstinence or mutual faithfulness in stable sexual relationships. If these options are not possible for some people, the proper and consistent use of latex condoms offers a high degree of protection against HIV and other sexually transmitted diseases (see pp.60-62, below).

3. Early diagnosis and treatment of other sexually transmitted diseases

Since infection with other sexually transmitted diseases greatly increases the risk of HIV transmission, early diagnosis and effective treatment of these diseases is an important method of risk reduction.

4. Safe blood transfusions

HIV can be transmitted in health-care settings by the transfusion of blood from infected to uninfected persons. This risk can be minimized by giving transfusions only when necessary, avoiding them in situations in which alternative treatments suffice. All blood to be transfused should be tested and found negative for antibodies against HIV.

5. Proper sterilization of needles and other skin-piercing instruments

Scalpels, needles, razor blades or traditional instruments which have been contaminated with HIV carry the risk of transmitting the virus if they are used to penetrate the skin of uninfected persons. Sterilization using standardized techniques can prevent this way of transmission.

Health-care institutions must establish strict policies and practices for the prevention of all nosocomial (hospital-acquired) infections.

6. Provision of sterile instruments for users of intravenously applied drugs

Needle-sharing by injecting drug users is another risk factor for HIV transmission. The availability of individual equipment for injecting, disinfection of equipment before usage and needle exchange programmes can remove the risk of transmission of HIV and of other blood-borne infections such as viral hepatitis B or C (see pp.62-63 below).

7. The link between care and prevention

Comprehensive physical, emotional and spiritual care for persons living with HIV/AIDS has been shown to be a very important and effective contribution to prevention. Appropriate care is a precondition for gaining their confidence and co-operation; and a comprehensive process of care helps families and communities to face the issues raised by HIV/AIDS and to consider and understand its implications for themselves (see pp.83-85 below).

8. *Reducing discrimination*

Stigmatization of persons because of their social status, sexual orientation or addiction to drugs makes them more vulnerable to risks, including the risk of infections. If such persons feel excluded and are afraid of having their identity revealed, they are less likely to seek care and counselling, to have access to health information and to co-operate with AIDS prevention programmes. Thus resistance to all forms of discrimination and advocacy for the rights of people who are vulnerable to HIV are not only ethical demands but also a contribution to effective prevention (see below, pp.58 and 74).

9. *Empowerment of persons who are particularly vulnerable*

Persons who have no power to make decisions about their own bodies in regard to sexual relationships are at a far greater risk of being infected with HIV, even if they have received effective education for prevention. This applies particularly to women, who must be empowered to resist cultural and economic pressures to engage in unwanted sexual relationships (see the "Ecumenical Platform of Action — Women's Health and the Challenge of HIV/AIDS", pp.17-18).

10. *Prevention of HIV transmission from mother to child*

Anti-viral treatment of pregnant women and their new-born children has recently been shown to reduce by about two-thirds the risk of vertical transmission. However, this treatment is not yet universally available because of its high cost.

Socio-economic and cultural contexts

Socio-economic and cultural contexts are determining factors in the spread of HIV/AIDS. Because these circumstances differ from place to place, countries, districts and even villages may have quite different HIV/AIDS stories and current profiles. But the WHO currently estimates that nine out of ten people with HIV live in areas where poverty, the subordinate status of women and children, and discrimination are prevalent.

Development practice with respect to HIV is paradigmatically the practice of human development. This is so for significant reasons. The focus of HIV is people's sexual, psychological and social relations and behaviour. No roads, fertilizers, procurement systems or stock exchanges are available to distract attention from or mask the fact that people are the focus of its practice.

It is critical to explore the relationship between economic, social and cultural variables and the spread of HIV — who becomes infected with the virus and with what spatial distribution. Examples which have been identified as having a causal role in the spread of the virus include gender (more specifically the economic, social and cultural lack of autonomy of women, which places them at risk of infection); poverty and social exclusion (the absence of economic, social and political rights); and labour mobility (which is more than the physical mobility of persons and includes the effects on values and traditional structures associated with the processes of modernization). At the core of the problem of transmission of HIV are issues of gender and poverty.

Thus, the classical components of development — transportation systems, labour markets, economic growth, governance, poverty and more — are within the causal framework which determines the patterns and speed of spread of the virus. These components will also be affected by the impact of the spread of the virus, its associated mortality and morbidity and the burden of dependency and social disruption it will create. No longer can the implications of failures to alleviate poverty or success in employment be understood in isolation. All of the components of development affect what happens with the HIV epidemic.

*Dr Elizabeth Reid, United Nations Development Programme,
HIV and Development Programme*

At the root of the global socio-economic and cultural problems related to HIV/AIDS are the unjust distribution and accumulation of wealth, land and power. This leads to various forms of malaise in human communities. There are more and more cases of economic and political migration of people within and outside of their own countries. These uprooted peoples may be migrant workers looking for better-paying jobs or refugees from economic, political or religious conflicts. Racism, gender discrimination and sexual harassment, economic inequalities, the lack of political will for change, huge external and internal debts, critical health problems, illicit drug and sex trades, including an increase in child prostitution, fragmentation and marginalization of communities — all these factors, which affect "developed" as well as "developing" societies, form a web of interrelated global problems which intensify the vulnerability of human communities to HIV/AIDS.

The family and AIDS

The family is a basic social unit of human relations. Through the family, persons are nurtured and sustained in mutual love and responsibility. In different places and circumstances the family exists in various forms: as a traditional nuclear family in a "household", or as an extended family, or as a family of choice. But whatever the form, HIV/AIDS touches the life, behaviour and perspectives of people in human families.

Human families are challenged continually by their socio-economic and cultural context, and by the phenomena of globalization and fragmentation, which contribute to the current fragility of human relationships. In many societies the fabric of family and community life is weakened by the imbalance of power between men and women — an imbalance which starts from the moment of birth. Often the "shared responsibility" for maintaining the social fabric falls on the shoulders of girls and women, who in many cultures however remain subordinate to men. To this imbalance of power is related the failure of men to take responsibility for issues related to sexuality, reproduction and HIV/AIDS.

Most people living with HIV/AIDS are in the prime productive and reproductive age group of 15 to 44 years. About half of all HIV infections occur among young people below 24 years of age, indicating the inherent vulnerability of youth in most cultures, a fact which is constant even though there are many different contexts within each culture.

An international ecumenical youth meeting held in Namibia in 1993 identified three of the biggest concerns for teenagers worldwide as relationships with peers, changing relationships with parents and families, and the experience of newly-found identities and sexuality. Young people feel the need to belong and to be accepted by those with whom they identify. Many of these relationships are creative, but peer pressure may lead to experimentation with sexuality and with the use of alcohol and drugs,[3] exposing them to HIV/AIDS risk factors. Often the problems are compounded by the attitudes and policies of community leaders. For example, a staff member of the WHO specializing in issues of youth and AIDS has noted that "the opposition of political and religious leaders (not to mention parents and teachers) to open and objective discussion of AIDS education for young people makes implementation of innovative and potentially effective interventions difficult, and sometimes impossible, worsening the situation".[4]

The vulnerability of young people, especially young women, reflects the current fragility of the roles constructed by each society for males and females from childhood on. Whenever gender discrimination leaves women under-educated, under-skilled and unable to gain title to property or other vital resources, it also makes them more vulnerable to HIV infection. In 1980 an estimated 80 percent of people living with HIV were men, and 20 percent were women. By the mid-1990s the number of women living with HIV had increased disproportionately; a recent estimate is that 40 percent of people living with HIV are women.

Economic, social and cultural factors which perpetuate the subordination of women are contributing to the spread of HIV. In many societies the position of women limits their control over their bodies and their power to make decisions about reproduction. Women may be forced into commercial sex work by their own economic situation or that of their families. Faced with overwhelming poverty, a woman who works in a brothel may reason: "If I work here I may die in ten years. If I do not, I will die of starvation tomorrow."

In addition, women's traditionally important role as care-giver within their families and communities exposes them in different contexts to the burdens of HIV/AIDS. Many are providing loving, supportive care to their sick husbands, children, parents and extended family. The overwhelming burdens of this nurturing role are not often shared by men. Thus women are usually the last to seek medical assistance; either the resources are no longer sufficient, or they have no time to attend to themselves or they are too exhausted to go for medical care. And in the case of pregnancy, lack of prenatal care makes it difficult for a woman with HIV to reduce the chances of infecting her children.

Ecumenical Platform of Action
Women's Health and the Challenge of HIV/AIDS

The HIV/AIDS epidemic is affecting all aspects of people's lives. Economic, social and cultural factors which perpetuate the subordination of women are contributing to the spread of the virus and exacerbating its effects on the lives of women. We acknowledge the excellent work that is being done in many situations, but in general, strategies of prevention and care by governments, churches and non-governmental organizations have so far failed to influence the broader determinants of the situation of women.

What has this to do with the churches?

Where the church is silent in the face of injustice in the lives of the people, it is not being faithful to God's mission. The time has come, then, for the church to examine and assess the extent of its complicity in upholding the social structures that perpetuate women's subordination.

In some parts of the world, for instance, the churches have collaborated in the myth that the transmission of the AIDS virus is confined to commercial sex workers, homosexuals and drug users. This is untrue and damaging, and needs to be refuted...

We are a group of thirty people from five continents... All of us have practical experience in working with church programmes related to HIV/AIDS. Some of us are living with HIV/AIDS... All of us had found that this work had continually challenged our thinking, our attitudes and our theology, and had transformed our vision. In sharing our experiences and the results of our research, we found that we do have much in common; that we gain strength and confidence by exchanging perspectives; and that the issues we face — though from widely differing contexts — were very much the same. We were able to reach unanimous agreement about an ecumenical platform of action.

Platform of Action

1. We call upon our churches to engage in self-critical examination of the churches' participation in and perpetuation of cultural biases and patterns that contribute to women's subordination and oppression.

2. We urge our churches to create an environment where the life experiences of women can be heard without fear of judgment, in an atmosphere of mutual love and respect, so that the issues that emerge may be addressed.

3. We strongly recommend that the churches re-evaluate the ways in which we have interpreted the Bible, along with church traditions and images of God. Many Christians have accepted these as truth without considering how far they are (or are not) rooted in

people's daily realities and consistent with the liberating message of Jesus.

4. We challenge the churches to acknowledge openly the sexual dimension of human experience and allow for this dimension to become part of ongoing church dialogue.

5. We commend this platform of action to our churches world-wide in the loving hope that they will remember always, in their consideration, reflection and prayers, that these issues do not have to do with abstract ideas but with real people, the quality of their lives and their well-being and health.

From a WCC AIDS Consultative Group workshop in Vellore, India, 7 September 1995

The Joint United Nations Programme on HIV/AIDS (UNAIDS) has reported that in high-prevalence countries with a long-standing epidemic, AIDS has begun to wipe out achievements in child survival, to shorten life expectancy and to threaten the very process of development.

Families are torn asunder by the pain which HIV/AIDS brings as children become orphans, and as men and women die in their most productive years. Grandparents who should be retiring find themselves caring for the sick, as this story from a remote village in Tanzania brings out vividly:

I visited an old man... He was a respected man, being one of the first ministers ordained in his church some decades ago. He told me that his two daughters had died of AIDS. Being a widower, he was now solely responsible for looking after four grandchildren. He had to provide food and clothing for them and to pay for the school fees of the eldest granddaughter.

Receiving a small pension from his church, he was a little bit better off than countless grandparents all over the world who have to look after their orphaned grandchildren nowadays. But his house, which had almost collapsed, the signs of malnutrition in his grandchildren and the resignation on his face showed that he could hardly cope with this additional burden at the end of his life.

NOTES

[1] *AIDS Epidemic Update*, UNAIDS/WHO, Dec. 2000.
[2] *Report on the Global HIV/AIDS Epidemic*, Joint United Nations Programme on HIV and AIDS (UNAIDS), June 2000.
[3] See Joao Guilherme Biehl, Janet Kenyon, Siv Limstrand and Anu Talvivaara, eds, *Making Connections: Facing AIDS, An HIV/AIDS Resource Book,* Geneva, WCC, Unit III and Lutheran World Federation Office for Youth, 1993.
[4] Chandra Mouli, Statement on "Youth and Aids: A Priority for Prevention", *Minutes of the First Meeting of the Consultative Group on AIDS (1994),* Geneva, WCC, Programme Unit II, 1995, p.69.

CHAPTER 3

Theological Perspectives

Within the churches, HIV/AIDS may raise anguished questions such as "Why does God allow the HIV virus to exist?" or "What is God doing about the epidemic?" or "What beliefs about God and human beings should inspire the churches' actions in response to HIV/AIDS?" In linking the medical and social context of the disease and its effects with belief in God, this chapter begins with the widest possible scope — a theology of creation — for it is only in the context of creation that the emergence of the HIV virus may be understood. Within God's creation live human beings, whose capacity for responding to relationship with God and each other, while remaining the social and sexual creatures they are, is critical.

Theology of creation

1. Relationships

Everything that is most valuable in a theology of creation may be expressed in terms of relationships. There are relationships within the Trinity; between God and creation, both its human and non-human aspects; among human beings; and between human beings and the natural world.

The life of the Holy Trinity moves in relationships among Father, Son and Holy Spirit, and characteristically all that God does in and with creation is also fashioned in the processes of relationships. Thus when God let the created world *be* (cf. Gen. 1:3), God did not let it *go*. The world was not left to survive on its own. Instead, at every moment the triune God initiates and maintains relationship with every part and particle of it. This is God's constancy, whether or not this divine action is recognized. But what does such action say about God? That question may be answered by exploring two primary characteristics of a good relationship and the consequences of each.

• *Freedom and the risk of evil.* No good relationship can be created by force, with the stronger party dominating the weaker. Relationships which endure and enhance are built on the respect of each for the other. Likewise, God, who makes and maintains relationships with creation, will not dominate or rule by force, since that would destroy any possibility of creation's response. Instead, God has given humanity freedom, so that people may choose relationship rather than be manipulated into obedience like puppets.

But women and men may use this divine gift of freedom, which is necessary for entering into real relationships with God, to deny any such relationship, indeed to deny all kinds of relationships. It is possible to prefer the comfort and advancement of the self — or the extended self in family or clan — to the possibilities of relationship. From that exclusive concentration on the self — "curving in on oneself", is how Luther described sin — comes the possibility of moral evil, the evil human beings do to each other.

What is true of human beings is also true in its own way of the non-human world: God chooses not to rule by force, but to allow the natural world to evolve as it can. Thus God is not to be blamed for earthquakes or volcanic eruptions: these arise in the course of the free development of the evolving world. Creation, including all gases, insects, plants and animals, is a multiplicity of co-existing finite freedoms which interrelate in complex ways. As the human species evolved, it has made its own impacts on the natural world, further complicating any attribution of cause and effect.

It is not surprising that from time to time this has given rise to natural evil, that is, suffering which comes from natural events. For example, when the earth's crust cooled, it formed freely into tectonic plates. In later times, when these plates rub up against each other, earthquakes occur and suffering may be caused. Again, out of the freedom which God gave to the natural world, some creatures have evolved which are injurious to others. The tsetse fly carries a parasite which may in turn produce disease in cattle. Thus the tsetse fly may bring about both animal and human suffering, but it is an entirely natural creature.

In just the same way, the possibility of the HIV virus has come out of the freedom which God has given the natural world to develop. It is injurious to humans and causes great suffering; yet for all the pain and problems that result, the virus is not something outside creation, nor is it a "special" creation of God's intended to punish human beings. Rather, it is something which has become possible as the world developed, a creature like everything else, and hence able to interact with contemporary conditions and to produce natural evil. God allows this to happen in spite of the misery it causes, but this is not an "intervention" on God's part. God will not remove the freedom given to the human and non-human creation. Out of a desire for real relationship, God will not use power to dominate and control; indeed, such behaviour would be foreign to God's own nature.

This is a partial description of God's relationship to what God has created. But if that were *all* one could say, it would not adequately describe a God of love.

• *The divine relationship of love.* If the first characteristic of a good relationship is respect for the otherness of the other and renunciation of domination, a second, equally important characteristic is the affection, love or esteem in which each holds the other. Only with that warmth of regard and sense of interconnectedness will the relationship blossom and flourish for both. Thus the Bible portrays a God of love, who "so loved the world..." (John 3:16), and beseeches women and men in their turn to love God and to walk in God's ways.

No creature is excluded from this love and this pilgrimage. If God's love had to be *earned* by what men and women do, no one would be worthy of it. But because it is given, everyone is included. All those who tend to be forgotten, excluded, denigrated or marginalized in every society in this world are never abandoned, because the divine relationship is constant. Even those who refuse this relationship are not cut off from the omnipresent love of God.

According to a theology of creation which takes account of these two points, God first takes the risk that the freedom of creation will produce moral or natural evil. Consequently, what women and men *do* with their freedom is of the utmost importance. Furthermore, in making relationships with all that is, God is not only open to the joy and flourishing of creation but also vulnerable to pain at its viciousness and disasters. So no matter what problems may arise out of the freedom of creation, God does not abandon it. Finally, although human and non-human creatures may have no choice but to suffer when the world in its freedom injures them, God has *chosen* out of love to accompany creation in all the changes of its precarious networks, seeking the finite response of creatures to the divine love.

2. Human beings in relation

To be human is to be in relation, to be involved in a web of connections with others — in the family, at work, in the church, at leisure. Above and beyond all this human relating is the relationship God freely offers to all in love. Relations with other human beings, like relations with God, may manifest the same respect for the otherness of the other which makes freedom possible, and the same warmth of relationship in the form of love.

Christians may speak confidently concerning God who is known in relationship because such a relationship of freedom and love was enacted visibly in Jesus Christ. During his life — which is as important for belief as his death, although it has had less attention in the Western theological tradition — Jesus showed in practice what it is to live this relationship with God, encountering others with the promise and demand of the kingdom.

There was in the way Jesus behaved an *openness* to people of all kinds, without barriers of class or race or gender. Just as God in love accompanies all creation, so Jesus went among the poor, telling them that they were loved by God even if they had not been able to keep the law scrupulously. He dined with a rich Pharisee, and told another who came to see him at night that he needed new vision and had to be born again (John 3:3). He healed Jewish lepers and a Roman soldier's child. There were women in the group that travelled with him, and unlike many holy men he did not shrink from the touch of a prostitute. In all that breadth of relationship, Jesus incarnated the *accessibility* of God, who "shows no partiality" (Acts 10:34; Rom. 2:11), but is open to all — rich or poor, sick or healthy, old or young.

When people and churches live out of relationship with God and follow Jesus, therefore, they will be continually open to others and offer relationship to them, even to those who seem very different. Just as there is no closing off of relationships in the gospel accounts of Jesus, so churches cannot withdraw into being congenial groups of the like-minded, refusing openness to and esteem for others who are physically or socially different.

A similar observation emerges from considering Jesus' relations with the religious establishment of his day. He attended the synagogue and was certainly no religious dissenter. But he denounced or by-passed religious practices and ordinances which put difficulties in the way of ordinary people in their relationship with God. Not only did he preach the immediacy of unconditional divine love and forgiveness, but he also put it into practice through his own accessibility and his going to where the people were. All this has something to say to the churches about human being-in-relation. It speaks powerfully against churches which confess that nothing separates *us* from the love of God (Rom. 8:39) — and then go on to set up barriers of their own between themselves and other people.

There can be no valuable relationship in which each does not desire the *well-being* of the others. God's concern for the well-being of creation is visible in Jesus' healing of the sick and his exorcising of demons. Medical work and forms of other healing maintain that tradition. This is one way human beings express both the openness, and the esteem and affection, of their being-in-relation to those with HIV/AIDS, even though no cure has been found.

Relationships continually require an enlargement of understanding. No one understands from the start everything about being in relation. It seems that this was the case even for Jesus. The gospels tell of Jesus' encounter with a Syrophoenician woman who asked for his help (Mark 7:24-30; Matt. 15:21-28). At first he answered that his calling was to Israel alone; but through this woman he came to understand that his ministry was to extend far more widely. Similarly, human beings in relation are always being called on to extend their understanding, especially when confronted by new situations such as that brought by the HIV/AIDS pandemic. Again Jesus, praying in the garden of Gethsemane that the cup of suffering might be taken from him, does not appear as one who is iron-clad in divine immunity, but rather as a person who went forward without the certainty of any such position and *trusted* in God. Nor are we required to be invulnerable and certain in our relationships. Rather we are called to be open, learning and trusting.

It is demanding to follow the way of Jesus in relationships. Such open being-in-relation, which acknowledges no barriers but seeks the well-being of all, will seldom be popular with the authorities. In political terms, Jesus was crucified because who he was and what he did represented a threat to the power which maintained public order as the Roman authorities saw it, and to the religious sensibilities of the Jewish leaders. Yet one understanding of the resurrection is to see in retrospect that no matter how abandoned and forsaken by God Jesus felt himself to be (Mark 15:34), God was present through it all and finally vindicated him. Not even the greatest misunderstanding or repression can separate those who are "on the way" from this sustaining love of God and from the fellowship of the church.

3. Sin, repentance and forgiveness

In our freedom, of course, it is possible to reject relationship with God and act as if this did not exist. It is equally possible to reject or disrupt relations with other human beings. Such distortion of being-in-relationship is *sin*. It comes about in relationships as selfishness works its way into action. Actions which harm others or the natural world are sinful, and we bear our share of responsibility for them.

This acknowledgment of human sinfulness has been expressed in a variety of ways in different church traditions and theologies. For example, the Orthodox churches, without denying the fact of human sinfulness, have emphasized the possibility of human perfection through spiritual growth. This *theosis* or "deification" depends on both God's grace and the human will. It is related to the human freedom to make choices which will lead in the end to greater union with God. As we are renewed by the Holy Spirit (cf. Titus 3:5) and continue to grow in our communion with God, our lives will show forth more of God's love and care. Protestant churches, on the other hand, have tended to emphasize the deep and pervasive persistence of sin, understood as the distortion of a right relationship with God, with other persons and with the natural order. They have stressed that this condition can be overcome only through justification — that is, the restoration of a right relationship with God — through Jesus Christ.

"All have sinned" (Rom. 3:23). No one escapes this situation. But a recognition of our common sinfulness may not only prevent feelings of personal superiority but also lead to mutual forgiveness and make spiritual growth possible. A story from the Desert Fathers illustrates such growth:

> A brother at Scetes committed a fault. A council was called to which Abba Moses was invited, but he refused to go. Then the priest sent someone to say to him: "Come, for everyone is waiting for you." So he got up and went. He took a leaking jug, filled it with sand, and carried it with him. The others came out to meet him, and said to him: "What is this, Abba?" The old man said to them: "My sins run out behind me, and I do not see them. And today I am coming to judge the errors of another?" When they heard this they said no more to the brother, but forgave him. [1]

One of the complaints against Jesus was that he forgave sins. Only God could do that, said his contemporaries. Yet to those who came to him with at least a little faith Jesus said, "Your sins are forgiven." Jesus forgave sins during his life: he did not have to die in order to do so. Thus Christians see both in his life and in his death the great affirmation that God forgives us, with all our accumulation of great and petty wrongdoing, all the failures of our relationships in the family, workplace and community, all the omissions, lies and excesses that pervade our human lives.

Jesus told a story about a steward who was forgiven over a large debt and then threw another servant into jail over a much smaller debt (Matt. 18:23-35). This is clearly not the behaviour hoped for from human beings-in-relation. Forgiveness enables a relationship to continue, but a refusal to forgive brings it to an end. Where there has been hurt, forgiveness is certainly not easy; and there are many situations related to the spread of HIV/AIDS in which relationships have been hurt and may take time to recover. True forgiveness — by God or by other human beings — never involves what Dietrich Bonhoeffer called "cheap grace". Yet it *is* gracious and it *does* make continuing relationship possible.

If churches are not to behave like the unforgiving steward, they have to become communities of the freely forgiven — communities of the healed which thus serve as places of healing for others. Churches of the forgiven are not in a position to reject or withhold relation from others. "Acceptance" in such a community is not a theoretical non-judgmentalism, but rather the enlarging experience of discovering who we all are-in-relation.

All this calls for repentance or *metanoia* as the proper personal reaction to a perception of what sin is really like in its horror and pain. Repentance does not *bring about* divine forgiveness of sin, as if that could be triggered by a human act. On the other hand, God's forgiveness, by which the relationship between God and human beings is maintained, precedes human repentance — although it is in repenting that the existence of forgiveness is discovered.

4. Punishment

A God who forgives in this way is not one who is concerned to *punish*. Neither the biblical account of creation nor the understanding of God gives any basis for attributing to God the desire for punishment. Moreover, when Jesus was invited to link sin with disaster, he refused utterly: "No, I tell you!" (Luke 13:3; cf. John 9:1-3). It may happen in private spirituality that the experience of HIV/AIDS may lead a person to repent of his or her own actions, as indeed other suffering may have this effect. But such a perspective on one's own actions is very different from believing that God, who is known in relationship and characterized by love, would deliberately send a punishment, let alone a punishment which falls more and more indiscriminately.

It is important to distinguish between *punishment* for an action and the *consequences* of an action. Consequences are the natural outcome of certain actions, the end result, to which several factors will have contributed. The outcome may be good or bad for the person or persons involved, but everything will have happened within "the way the world goes", and in the freedom God gave it. To speak of an event as "punishment" from God, however, attributes to God a requirement for retribution — as if divine morality were "an eye for an eye and a tooth for a tooth" — and a readiness, in pursuit of this retribution, to disrupt human or natural life by intervening in it.

A case study may make clearer the way in which actual events always involve a complex *constellation of causes and consequences*, rather than a single cause and effect, and thus underscore the problems and limitations involved in labelling consequences as "punishment".

Consider the following situation: A young girl from the hill tribes of northern Thailand leaves her family to find a job in the big city of Bangkok. Her parents urge her to do so, because — as subsistence farmers whose produce commands a very low price — they cannot survive without additional income. In Bangkok the girl is put into a brothel where many girls are held in captivity by the wealthy owner. Most of the money from the clients goes to him, but the young girl does manage to send small amounts of money to her family at home. The brothel is regularly visited by rich men from Bangkok and by sex tourists from abroad who abuse the girls for their personal pleasure. The HIV infection rate among the girls is very high, as many of the clients are HIV-infected and pass the virus on to them — and they, in turn, pass it on to other clients.

Clearly there are many factors at work here: there is no simple process of cause and effect. Sinful structures in society are involved — economic conditions which virtually force the parents to sell their daughter into slavery, and sinful behaviour on the part of many people, including the brothel owner, clients and tourists who regard the girls not as human beings but as commodities or objects. At each point in the story, relationships are broken and disrespected.

This shows why it is socially, ethically and theologically impossible to link sin directly with punishment. If the girl were infected with HIV by a sex tourist, that would be a consequence, indeed a bad one, but given the circumstances of her background it cannot be regarded as "punishment" for being a prostitute. If, on the other hand, the sex tourist caught the infection from the girl, that would again be a consequence of the encounter. But who is to say what circumstances have led to his behaviour, or have discouraged him from living out his sexuality in a responsible way in a mutually faithful relationship? This is not to deny that some actions are better than others, or that people are always in some degree responsible for what they do. But it does suggest that once the background and all the circumstances of an individual are understood — as God *does* — then it is evident that the labelling of certain consequences as "punishment" for certain actions is inappropriate.

The World Council of Churches' executive committee emphasized in its 1987 statement the need "to affirm that God deals with us in love and mercy and that we are therefore freed from simplistic moralizing about those who are attacked by the virus".[2] The terminology of punishment should be rejected in favour of an understanding of God in omnipresent, constant, loving relationship, no matter how much some of the actions of every one of us may grieve God. A moralistic approach can easily distort life within the Christian community, hampering the sharing of information and open discussion which are so important in facing the reality of HIV/AIDS and in inhibiting its spread. The response of Christians and the churches to those affected by HIV/AIDS should rather be one of love and solidarity, expressed both in care and support for those touched directly by the disease, and in efforts to prevent its spread.

5. Acceptance

Christ's community of care is an environment in which risks can be taken, all members accept mutual vulnerability and stories may be shared in trust and commitment to each other. Unfortunately, many churches do not offer such a safe place for people living with HIV/AIDS. All too often the knowledge that a person is HIV-positive results in gossip and rejection.

In a community of care, by contrast, "acceptance" moves from a simple avoidance of being judgmental to an embracing of who we are individually and, more importantly, together — the difference between receiving someone into your home as a guest, who remains "other", and embracing someone as a rightful member of the family.

The presence of HIV in our community — particularly, but not exclusively, in the church community — requires this shift in our understanding of acceptance. We are not called simply to offer charity to those whose physical bodies have the virus. Our undeniable belonging to the community challenges us to embrace the fact, however painful, that the virus has come into *our* body.

The parable of the prodigal son (Luke 15:11-32) is a rich story about acceptance. Its characters depict contrasting attitudes similar to those which many of us hold, often simultaneously, about HIV. But we must be careful from the outset not to make comparisons in terms of "blame" between the prodigal son and persons living with HIV/AIDS, for this would reflect a misunderstanding of the virus and how it is transmitted.

God's love and compassion are certainly not restricted to Christians, nor to those whom Christians might deem "worthy". Yet we often respond like the elder son, who self-righteously resents that

God's love, compassion and concern are shared generously with all. What is required in regard to HIV/AIDS is the attitude of the father, who meets his son with unconditional love without reference to the son's behaviour.

It is the younger son who begins with acceptance — of himself, his situation and his need for reconciliation. His action challenges his father to receive him home and to accept him as a son. In mutual acceptance, right relationship is restored and healing begun.

Similarly, we must first accept that HIV affects us as a community. Then, in mutual relationships with those whose bodies are infected, healing can begin. Such healing will include the restoration of relationship with ourselves, with others and with God.

A community of this kind will provide the environment for a mutual sharing of our stories. This is a process towards real conversion (*metanoia*) for all involved, a process in which the whole community, through moments of genuine vulnerability, offers and receives the gifts of each person in love and acceptance.

Human sexuality

Sexuality is an integral part of human identity. It is expressed in a variety of ways, but finds particular expression in intimate human relationship. It is "erotic" in the classic sense, that is, it drives one to move beyond oneself into encounter with another in relationship. And while this aspect of human identity finds particular expression in the dimension of physical intimacy, it cannot be separated from its emotional, intellectual, spiritual and social dimensions. A Christian understanding of sexuality seeks to take account of the fullness of all these dimensions, yet recognizes the mystery which God has given to human beings in sexuality as a whole.

Christianity has traditionally understood sexuality to be a gift of God for the task of procreation. In some traditions this is linked with an understanding of human beings as "co-creators" with God. While the role of sexuality in procreation is clear, a broader understanding of sexuality also values its role in enriching partnership between persons and in bringing pleasure. Society has therefore come to recognize a diversity in the types of human sexual relationships and continues to face questions, for example, about the acceptance of non-heterosexual identity.

Along with its potential for bringing the richness of intimacy and joy to human relationships, sexuality makes people particularly vulnerable — to each other and to social forces. In connection with HIV/AIDS, sexuality increases vulnerability in two ways. First of all, as we have seen, many physical expressions of sexuality can bring one into contact with HIV infection. Second, the very fact that humans are sexual beings makes them vulnerable to the many and varied social factors which influence moral decisions and actions.

Like other aspects of creation, sexuality can be misused if people do not recognize their personal responsibility. Thus societies have always sought to protect people from vulnerability in this area. Through value systems which classify certain behaviours as socially unacceptable or through more formal means such as the institution of marriage, the expression of human sexual desire has been regulated and directed in ways deemed necessary for responsible and safe community life. Churches have particularly affirmed the role of marriage in this regard. In spite of all these attempts to provide protection and encourage responsibility, the abuse of sexual power and relations remains a reality. This is particularly apparent in the growing commercialization of sex and in sex tourism.

The AIDS virus is fragile. For its transmission it depends upon intimate contact. And there is an interesting connection between intimacy and vulnerability. Every intimate contact makes us vulnerable in all sorts of ways, not only through transmission of infection but also psychologically and in our personal identity. This is why every civilization has in various ways surrounded intimate relationships with rules, with structures, with ceremonies, with taboos. These have, as it were, protected the relationships.

What I see the AIDS epidemic as teaching us is that we can no longer treat these intimate relationships lightly. That is where the world has lost its sense that close contact between human beings needs to be within an ordered framework... This, it seems to me, is a moral and theological understanding which can be expressed in ways which are accessible not only to those with Christian commitment but to all those who think seriously about our human nature and our contacts with one another.

Archbishop of York John Habgood, speaking at a hearing on AIDS during the WCC central committee meeting in January 1987

But ideas of what is sexually moral (that is, of what is "right" and not "wrong") are formed in a constant interaction between personal and community values. There is continuing debate about the origins of sexual *identity*, that is, whether it is genetically "given" or learned through social development. But it is certain that belief in, and adherence to, moral *behaviour* are developed in social interaction.

Christian faith and the churches clearly have an important role in influencing how this interaction occurs, and in the development of personal and community beliefs. In many instances Christianity and other religions have helped to develop, if not determine, prevailing systems of social moral responsibility. A case in point, as noted earlier, is the affirmation of the primary nature of marriage in building family and community.

Although the ongoing intra-confessional and ecumenical discussion about sexual orientation cannot be resolved here, it is important to recognize the role churches play in determining the environment in which people — often those with whom churches may disagree — are affected by HIV/AIDS. At times theological differences must be put

---

Orthodoxy is quite clear on this point: the sexual life of men and women is possible only in marriage, the purpose of which is procreation. Throughout the Christian world, marriage has become so unstable that it now seems almost unnecessary. In Russia, almost half of marriages break up, leaving about half a million children without one parent every year. Sixty percent of men and forty percent of women commit adultery, and infidelity ranges from one-time unfaithfulness to creation of a second and even a third family on the side. It is in this age that children enter sexual relations nowadays. The young people who do not want to marry entertain themselves sexually, corrupting their own bodies and souls. To speak nowadays about sexual restraint before marriage is something abnormal and even "amoral".

Meanwhile, marriage is God's institution. Orthodoxy has always taught that marriage has a great calling and regarded it as God's will and the fulfillment of one's earthly duty, which is procreation and propagation of Christian faith on earth.

Anatoly Berestov, Russian Orthodox Church,
WCC consultative group on AIDS meeting,
Geneva, September 1994

aside in light of the imperative to prevent human suffering and to care for those who are suffering. The churches' role in developing moral decision-making skills is a key to this.

Churches have not always encouraged open and affirming discussion of issues of human sexuality. But if sound moral decisions are required of people, an environment conducive to making such decisions is necessary, an environment in which openness to honest sharing of experiences and concerns is promoted and the integrity of people and their relationships is affirmed. Apart from such an environment, the vulnerability of marginalized groups to high-risk behaviour is greatly increased.

Gay men, who were among the first to be affected by the pandemic and often play a very significant role in care and prevention, have frequently been condemned and marginalized by the churches. Some have argued that religious communities which have contributed to this marginalization bear some responsibility for the increased vulnerability of these persons, and that both parties must enter into a new relationship to make for more effective prevention and mutual care.

Of the many factors related to the pandemic, sexuality has perhaps received the least attention in ecumenical discussion. Further study in this area is essential for a deeper understanding of the challenges posed by HIV/AIDS.

A theology of suffering and death, hope and resurrection

Our lives and the whole of creation are held within the love of God in Christ. As Christians we live from the promise that nothing can separate us from God's love: no tragedies, accidents or disasters, no disease of body or mind, no personal actions, thoughts or feelings, no global structures of injustice and oppression, no natural or supernatural powers: nothing, not even death, can break God's solidarity with us and with all creation (Rom. 8:38-39).

We are also promised entry into God's final purpose for our lives and all creation. This is life abundant, a life in which each has enough and justice reigns, a life of fulfillment in which we can explore in security all the gifts God has given us. This promise shines through the Bible, from the varied accounts of creation (Gen. 1-3), to the words of the prophets (Isaiah 25) to the vision of the heavenly city

(Rev. 21-22). This is creation's *birthright*, the "glory" for which God has destined humanity and all of creation.

But within this framework of God's final vision for humanity and creation is another experience. For we do not live in a world in which there is no death, sorrow, crying and pain (Rev. 21:3). The way to glory evidently leads through suffering: for in spite of all the joy and beauty life has to offer, there is much sorrow, injustice, tragedy and waste. Some of this we can understand as the consequences — for ourselves and for others — of our own acting in the freedom given us by God; some we cannot immediately understand, though we sense that it may belong to a larger pattern of which we now glimpse only a part. But some suffering, sorrow and injustice we cannot understand at all; and we cry out, "I believe; help my unbelief!" (Mark 9:24).

But it is not only we who suffer in this world; the world also suffers in this world. The whole creation, for all its beauty and the marvellous order which it reveals, groans in "labour pains" (Rom. 8:22). Both living beings and nonliving material objects are subject to decline and decay. There is disease and illness. Many creatures live — and *can* live — only at the expense of others: indeed, many can live only through the *death* of others. The natural world is racked by equally "natural" disasters. Is this also an expression of the freedom God has given God's "creatures"? And for all their diversity, all living things without exception are united in facing a common lot: their lives in their present form will end in death.

The promise of God is strong and true. But it is hardly surprising that from time to time some of us are overwhelmed, confused or angry in the face of mysteries which test our faith in the faithfulness of God.

In such moments we experience the Spirit within us, calling us again to the mystery and "madness" of our faith, speaking for us when we cannot find the words, giving us courage to stand with others despite our own discouragement and fear, calling the church to be what it is: the body of Christ, broken for others in love. It is the Spirit which calls us to hear God's promise again, and frees us to hear it anew, opening us to hope (Rom. 8:15,24-26).

Finally we live by hope, for our questions and doubts are held within the larger frame of God's love and promise for us and for the whole of creation. We confess that we are not alone. We suffer with Christ — who is "God with us", Immanuel — "so that we may also be glorified with him" (Rom. 8:17). Christ who has gone before us into glory is the basis for our hope. Christ is present with us in our suffering and struggle, not as one who offers a simple answer to every question but as the inspiration and pattern on our way. And in our weakness we are sustained by the Spirit who dwells in us (Rom. 8:11), interceding when we do not know how to pray (v.26) and finally granting life to our mortal bodies (cf. Eph. 3:16).

As Christ identifies with our suffering and enters into it, so we are called to enter into the suffering of others. Remembering the Suffering Servant (Isa. 42:1-9; 49:1-7; 50:4-11; 52:13-53:12), we are called to share the sufferings of those living with HIV/AIDS, opening ourselves in this encounter to our own vulnerability and mortality.

As Christ has gone before us through death to glory, we are called to receive the sure and certain hope of the resurrection. This is God's promise that God's promise, for us and for all creation, is not destroyed by death: that we are held within the love of God, claimed by Christ as his own and sustained by the Spirit; and God will neither forsake us nor leave us to oblivion.

The early Christian texts envision and express this hope in various complementary ways. Some speak of a new quality and intensity of life, infusing our present existence and transforming it with new meaning (John 5:24; 10:10). Other texts speak of a new existence after this present life — of our being raised to eternal life at the "last day" (John 6:39-40) or awakening from sleep to new life in a "resurrection body" whose seed was sown at death (1 Cor. 15:35-58). But all strands of the early Christian tradition affirm the bedrock conviction that God, through the power of the Spirit, gives new life in Christ, a life which is stronger than death.

The experience of faith in the face of suffering despair, the search for healing and salvation, the expectation of death, the hope of resurrection

Ernesto Barros Cardoso

Doing theology on the basis of foundations and epiphanies
My spiritual education always reinforced, during adolescence, the importance of faith as the certainty of certain foundations, a

specific base and structure. To have faith was always, at that time of my life, trust and total surrender "into the hands of God" and the acquisition of principles and values, concepts and affirmation that guided me and made me a multiplier, interested in "speaking of Jesus" to friends and strangers. On a number of occasions, what inspired me was the parable of the two houses and their respective foundations: sand and rock (Matt. 7:24-27).

For five years I have been living in a house in a peaceful area in the outskirts of Rio de Janeiro, a fishing village. The house is spacious but its construction is simple and rather crude, not at all sophisticated. It is hard to fathom the process of construction and the logic of the builder. It is the kind of house that has been enlarged and renovated bit by bit — through momentary decisions, using space without ever having followed a plan, probably.

The work I have done on the house has taught me to pay great attention to this detail. It is difficult to make any changes in the furnishings of the house, but when I contemplate making the space more efficient or adapting it to some new situation — out of a creative impulse or aesthetic sense; when I want to change the use of the basics in order to emphasize other characteristics and details which habit, boredom and repetitive action have made to disappear from sight, then the task becomes even more difficult.

I can remember a children's game with a large number of small pieces and gears that had to be put together into a shape and sometimes made to move. A variety of solutions using basic elements... something like 1001 creative possibilities?

Classical theology and the classical way of doing theology reinforce the importance of affirmation and certainties, of bases and foundations, of the security that springs from consensus. In the biblical tradition, a national, institutional, messianic theology, produced during the era of reconstruction after the return from exile, affirmed faith in the foundations and in security as a way of overcoming times of instability and vulnerability. To the present day, biblical images, repeated in theological textbooks and in the poetry of traditional hymns (the hands of God, the Rock, the Foundation, Mount Zion that is never shaken, the anchor that holds against all the forces of the sea and the tempest), reinforce the experience of the Sacred as relationship to the immutable.

But can theology be conceived as a *risky* and *contingent* activity — as in the declaration of faith by the father who went to find Jesus to cure his daughter: "I believe, help me in my lack of faith" (Mark 9:24)? To find a genuine expression of faith in the face of abandonment and doubt, it is worth looking back to the expression of Abraham, Jacob, Moses, Job. The Psalms also portray these instants of faith in the midst of crisis and lack of prospects or meaning: "Why do you not hear me, Lord? Why do you turn away?" Some prophets said this situation of abandonment and distance from God was the result of the people's sin, the nation's sin. Sometimes they used the metaphor of prostitution, which meant fleeing to other forms of security, trying to maintain political and economic power through bogus alliances, turning away from the pure gratuitousness of "serving Yahweh" and "surrendering into his hands" in complete trust.

It is appreciably different to emphasize the base, the structure, as what is relevant, significant, essential. Value resides in the structure, the foundations, and therefore in their invariableness, immutability, inflexibility and rigidity — like the stone, the rock, Mount Zion that is not shaken. But what a difference it would make to recognize the importance of structure and foundation precisely because of the rich *possibilities* they offer to open up — on that structure or base — to new creations and interpretations, to successive epiphanies and expressions that inspire and sharpen sensibility, that stimulate vision, that call for a new gesture, renewing commitment, enabling a permanent "conversion" or metanoia. All of this is far from the inflexible and repetitive speeches which do not convince precisely because of the monotony of their forms and methods.

The experience of faith in times that "melt into air"

Doing theology in the 20th century has been a arduous task and has for a number of reasons grown more so: the acceleration of change at the end of the millennium and related concern about what is to come over the next decades; the weakness of categories and paradigms; the "pasteurization" of cultural processes, which attacks differentiation that becomes radicalism and sectarianism.

Despite the diversity of readings and responses, we live on the other hand with a great deal of accommodation to the processes of globalization. There is also a great silence about and a certain complicity with the imposition of neo-liberal models and global solutions, not only in economics and politics, but also in culture. Communities of faith, theological seminaries and ecumenical centres are slow to stay in tune and maintain a sense of timing with the changes. There are crucial issues, and the situation of AIDS with its impact on societies and cultures is only one example of the difficulty of response, experimentation, the construction of languages and visions.

Theology from the standpoint of the body that suffers and dreams and delivers itself up to the Mystery

It is hard not to speak in the first person singular. I do not think this implies reductionism or exaggerated individualism. Every time we pay attention to individual experience, we can identify elements that are more general, collective.

That is the case with the suffering body. When my infections became acute in recent years, the immediate sensation was of identification through my body with the bodies of so many other people, in anonymity and solidarity; with — somehow — the suffering and the limits to energy and to resistance to pain.

In a way, the suffering led me to recognize the limits of my body. There was a kind of division between the pace of thought and awareness — a quicker one, more hopeful, trying to get around limits — and the lack of control over legs and feet, over the body in pain, over the unexpected sleepiness and intermittent diarrhoea.

The experience accentuated the same feeling of weakness, fragility, vulnerability, mortality reflected in certain compositions by contemporary artists like Freddy Mercury, George Michael and Sting. Or the controversy caused by the curator of the 1995 Venice Biennale, the French art critic and historian Jean Clair. The theme was "Identity and Otherness: A Brief History of the Body", and according to Clair, the exhibition would be quite gloomy, "maybe because we are at the end of a century, and both art and society are living through a morbid period..." One commentator said that "morbidity is an elegant way of saying horror. One can wonder: why does the end of a century have to bring with it so many cadavers, deformed faces, diseases, physical unhappiness?"... An exhibition of the decadence and deterioration of the human project as this century ends. Profound contradictions.

As a normal response to the pain and despair of experiencing limits, a profound cry sometimes, in silence or in tears, a murmur that seems like Paul's image of all of creation groaning as if in the pangs of childbirth as it awaits its liberation from limits and vulnerability (cf. Rom. 8). A sensation of the collective unconscious: in one body, all bodies. The individual experience that can create bonds of solidarity, feel one with all bodies that suffer. Maybe this is close to one of the songs of the suffering servant: "Surely he has borne our infirmities and carried our diseases; yet we accounted him stricken, struck down by God and afflicted" (Isa. 53:4). In one body, all bodies. The tired, suffering body of the world, the oppressed and downtrodden body of the poor, the repressed and violated body of so many women, the bodies, without energy and resistance, of boys and girls...

It is impossible not to have the feeling, in spite of the particularity of my experience, of identifying with millions. Yes, we are millions who are *infected* and *affected*.

Cure, destiny, salvation

In the face of the pain and suffering, the first solution that suggests itself is a cure: stopping suffering, putting an end to pain, recovering the energy, "coming back to life". As a cure is hard to come by or, in AIDS cases, impossible, the idea of some kind of miracle emerges very strongly. A fantastic solution, perhaps, but what can be said of the many cures in biblical narratives, or associated with the ministry of service (*diakonia*) and healing?

From the first time I heard my diagnosis, I wondered why I should be or should want to be cured. What about the millions of others? Would there be a cure for everyone? Would the miracle reach us all? And why? Would it solve the problem for everyone?

Here the questions about destiny and predestination and about the consequences or wages of sin arise again. Or perhaps it is a trial, a test. The same disturbing questions that Job asked come up again and often elicit the same not very good advice as was offered by his friends in the biblical account. The same experience of abandonment and meaninglessness. If not as many cures happen as are necessary, is it a question of increasing the number of people who heal and pray? Is it a question of each person's faith? Is it a question about God's "plan"? Is it a trial or predestination?

Personally I understood miracles and cures like those described in the gospels as signs of divine possibility, of God's ultimate desire to reintegrate people's lives in terms of personal fulfilment, happiness, integration with social group and family, citizenship and bodily dignity. Jesus' gestures seemed like *epiphanies*. The fantastic and the unusual were indications of these possibilities of salvation (*shalom*) specific to messianic times, to the kingdom of God. They were expressions of the "madness" (or "foolishness", as the apostle Paul says in 1 Cor. 1:18-31?) of faith, of what it is worth risking one's life for — that which is really essential.

Why should there be a cure for me if I know that millions will not be cured? Here we see the collapse of the theological concept of a God who makes choices, assigning a cure to some and suffering to others. What God have we constructed in the end? In the name of what God do we work? How many ridiculous and scandalous things have been seen in the "divine cure" section of certain churches and sanctuaries!

About "destiny": the Greek expression for this idea — or power — that governed the lives of everyone, even the gods, was *moira*. José Américo Pessanha, a philosopher from Rio de Janeiro, recalls that

> *moira* originally had a spatial meaning. It is the feeling of one's own space, province, jurisdiction, parish, the territory a person can occupy. When someone lives life until the end, that person has opened out in space all of what he or she was able to be. Therefore, a second meaning of the word "destiny" is linked to "end"; a person arrives at his or her limit or end, which is identified with death. Only with death does life's space show itself fully. Life is a conquest of space that broadens and with death gains its final shape. So *moira*, destiny, is that mapping, that acreage, the lot that each person occupied (in Fayga Ostrower, *Acasos e cração artística*, p.5).

And that makes me think about eternal life. Is it real? Will it be a gift? Is it a condition for hope? Or is it like an extra, assuming life —

whatever the length — but soaking it in meaning, adding quality to it, giving it profundity by the intimate relationship to mystery that engenders and maintains it? Are these ways of "filling the space" (*moira*) and "fulfilling destiny"?

Mystery and grace — hope and resurrection

John of the book of Revelation dreamed of a land without evil or tears and of a tent set up for God to affirm God's constant presence and company (cf. Rev. 21:22). He conceived faith as a paradise that was found less in longing for the past than in hope (utopia). The key to understanding hope seems to me this courage or energy to throw oneself into Mystery, the Sacred, what is beyond!...

This is counter to that idea of a human plan to "build the kingdom of God" which has been pervasive in our theological centres and from our pulpits since the 1950s or 1960s. Again, the images of the Venice Biennale indicate the bankruptcy of the 20th-century project for civilization and the degradation of the human race.

The gospels present the kingdom in signs, gestures, indications, insights, first-fruits. So they point to a situation in which — even if as the first-fruits, as an aperitif — the quality of life, the defence of the dignity of life and of people, of their integrity, can be experienced not as *struggle*, which must lead to the naming of winners, of new holders of power (albeit in the name of the people, of democracy). Rather, the challenge of the kingdom is closer to an anti-power, an anti-institution, to the madness of faith, of hope against all hope (the hope of Abraham). The kingdom manifests itself — its epiphanies come — in gestures, rituals and oracles without pretensions to universality or global plans and strategies. These manifestations occur in different cultural contexts, simultaneously and successively, as a response of faithfulness by men and women who rush into the "mystery", sharpen their senses to discover these "epiphanies" and do theology as *pure sensibility*, as expression of dependence and surrender.

Rational questions cannot be asked of the mystery of life and death. That road leads nowhere. In the face of the Mystery, what is possible is simply to flow along, to let go, to throw oneself in like little turtles that are born in the sand and move down to the immense sea and let themselves go.

Cazuza, a Brazilian composer who died of HIV/AIDS, used to sing: "Crazy life, brief life, immense life... if I can't take you along, I want you to take me."

The Mystery cannot be translated into words and rationalizations. Theological formulations in the classical mode usually take a scandalous distance from daily life, from contradictory and critical situations, from bodies that are on the margins of social and cultural experience, economically and politically excluded and discriminated against. Unfortunately, this classical theology — and its "rules" as taught to new "theologians" — always return to the same refrains, the same words and round phrases, very good arguments, very well-reasoned, strictly following the models of the humanities and social sciences. Philosophical arguments...

I wonder what further action would be necessary to perceive this contact with the Mystery and the whole range of unheard-of and unusual situations, and the perplexity they cause in the mutilated and suffering bodies seeking hope and signs of resurrection. I remember the absurd amount Job suffered and how, at the end of his experience of doing theology with his own body, he learned to reject rationalizations imposed as truths. I also remember what his friends said was "the foundation", "the basis" of arguments, and how they said that he should trust them, accept the pain, confess his sin and, who knows, be forgiven and cured! At the end of his experience, when he sees the Sacred in all its grandeur, Job collapses and says: "I had heard of you by the hearing of the ear, but now my eye sees you" (Job 42:4).

Hope and resurrection are intimately related to his profound experience of faith. This confrontation usually does not find words and arguments that can express its impact. A radical change of perception, of view and of projection:

In the face of the drama of so many bodies walking,
seeking a home a shoulder, an embrace,
a meaning that helps to understand this pain, to face it,
and go beyond resignation...
and then integrate it as a part of life experience,
of exercising the limits imposed, daring to advance
and extend the margins imposed by illness...

I think the attitude of the leadership of the churches, its thinkers (theologians) and its ministers (deacons and pastors), should help these people — the multitude of homeless, roofless, shelterless, family-less, energy-less, future-less people — to recover and to re-encounter, from within their pain and their suffering body, the responses and arguments, the inexhaustible spring that helps to make radical changes. Only confrontation with the Mystery, with the always-open revelation of God, can break down the faith in well-prepared speeches which — for that very reason — no longer "convince" many people.

Now is when symbols, gestures, indirectness, silence are fundamental: learning to do liturgy with people who suffer, learning to discover signs of the Sacred in the midst of garbage and dregs, learning to recognize this "holy land" in order to remove one's sandals and, in silence and profound expectations, to meet like Moses what is "further beyond"!

I think that the most profound experience for the sufferer who does not find a reason for suffering, who gets lost in the many questions and recipes for alleviating pain and curing the woes of body and soul, who is overwhelmed by advice from inept friends and empty talk, is precisely *living* a totally new experience based on a change in approach and perspectives, on openness to the newness of the revelation of God. This is something like being born again, being born in the Spirit: finding deeply, in solidarity and companionship, this Spirit of all bodies and of all creation, who echoes the moans and clamours (Rom. 8) while awaiting the utopia of resurrection.

In its radicality, however, this experience is very fragile. It is like throwing oneself into the wind, into unpredictable movements, for this is how the Spirit is (cf. John 3:8: "you do not know where it comes from or where it goes"). What we have is just the effect of its passing, the effect of movement! Who has eyes to see and ears to hear...? Being "born in the Spirit" results from this jumping into the air or the wind like a hang-glider in free flight — or diving into the rapids or the ocean waves and "letting oneself go".

I remember children's games with soap bubbles: the lightness and fragility of the bubble, the careful filling it with air and detaching it from the straw to see it fly away free in the wind, the desire to extend the palm of one's hand to "hold up" the bubble — almost always impossible. The same often happened with the balloons filled with air or helium that we had at parties as children: Would they burst? Would they float away? There was a magic that moved us as we weighted the "lightness" of air in the midst of such vulnerability and fragility.

I have learned, with some difficulty and not without suffering, to exercise actively my experience of faith. This confrontation with my body — and with all bodies in solidarity, on the limits and at the margins — and with the spiritual dimensions of my own existence gives me redoubled attention, a sharpened sensibility. From what I have seen, lived and experienced, I understand that theology and ethics are built like this, woven in the midst of existence, a constant epiphany, revelation. A fragile, contingent process that confronts life itself and the possibility of discovering in the midst of many risks (the bubble will pop, the balloon will not fly) a new rationality, of finding values regarding the base and substance of faith that have been lost or covered over by time, a technique that is more perfect than "jumping into the air" — a matter of permanent conversions, this unheard-of and unusual conviviality of traditions and modernity, of foundations and epiphanies.

Then we come closer and closer to really pricking up our ears, focusing our eyes, sharpening our imagination and exercising new languages — to allowing ourselves to take the risk in the midst of symbols, words and sounds, colours, silences, memories of life, and to celebrate the Mystery of life. As Lulu Santos and Nelson Motta have written in *"Como uma onda"* ("Like a Wave"):

Nothing that was will be
again in the ways it once was

> *everything will pass*
> *everything will always pass...*
>
> *life comes in waves like the sea*
> *in an infinite to and fro*
> *all that is seen*
> *is not the same that we saw*
> *a second ago*
>
> *everything changes all the time everything in the world*
> *there is no point pretending*
> *or lying to ourselves*
>
> *now, there is so much life out there*
> *in here*
> *always*
> *like a wave in the sea.*
>
> *Ernesto Barros Cardoso, a member of the WCC AIDS consultative group, wrote this text during and just after his hospitalization in 1995 for AIDS-related opportunistic infections. These led to his death following a further hospitalization in late 1995.*

The body of Christ, the human body and HIV/AIDS

As the body of Christ, the church is to be the place where God's healing love is experienced and shown forth and God's promise of abundant life is made freely available. In making tangible the love and care of Christ, the church offers a prophetic sign and foretaste of the kingdom. In its confession, proclamation, worship and service, the church is called to witness to the presence of Christ in the world.

Christ's offer of abundant life is to be made available to all. The inclusiveness of Christ is especially seen in his parables about meals, such as that of the great banquet pictured in Luke 14:15-24, with their emphasis on the generosity of God's invitation, which does not discriminate among those invited on grounds of their merits, abilities, beliefs or moral standing.

Because all persons fall within the scope of God's love and are honoured with Christ's care, we are called to honour one another as if in each person we encounter Christ himself. When we fail to honour the icon and image of the divine which we should see in ourselves and in our neighbours, then we are not being true to our calling as members of Christ's body, the church.

As Christ identifies with our suffering and enters into it, so the church as the body of Christ is called to enter into the suffering of others, to stand with them against all rejection and despair. This is not an option; it is the church's *vocation*. And because it is the body of *Christ* — who died for all and who enters into the suffering of all — the church cannot exclude anyone who needs Christ, certainly not those living with HIV/AIDS.

In opening itself to persons living with HIV/AIDS, in entering into their suffering and bearing it with them, in standing with them against rejection and despair, the church expresses more fully what it is to be the body of Christ. And as the church enters into solidarity with persons living with HIV/AIDS, its hope in God's promise of abundant life comes alive and becomes visible to the world.

Some churches are showing courage and commitment in manifesting Christ's love to persons affected by HIV/AIDS. Other churches have contributed to stigmatizing and discriminating against such persons, thus added to their suffering. The advice of St Basil the Great comes to all those in leadership positions within the church, emphasizing their responsibility to create an environment — an ethos, a "disposition" — in which the cultivation of love and goodness can prevail within the community and issue in that "good moral action" which is love.[3]

The church is called to stand with persons who are affected by HIV/AIDS. This "standing with", this service of the church on behalf of those who suffer, will take different forms in each situation depending on the needs and possibilities. In some cases the church will need to work for better medical care for affected persons; in other cases, to work for improved counselling services, or for the defence of basic human rights, or to ensure that accurate factual information is available within the church and to the general public, or to ensure that a climate of understanding and compassion prevails. Most of the time all of these efforts and more will be needed.

In the incarnation, God in Christ has entered into the world, breaking down the barriers between the spiritual and the material, claiming the material world as a place where God is present and active for good. Thus, in the incarnation,

> matter has itself become at least potentially sacred, the vehicle of the divine. The very stuff of creation is revelatory and is to be celebrated...

Matter is sacramental, instinct with the divine and, when used aright, it is a vehicle of the divine presence, the outward and visible becoming the effective sign of the invisible but real mystery of God.[4]

Our response to God in this life is inseparable from our physical participation in the life of the world. To deny this participation by devaluing the material and physical world reflects a failure to understand the incarnation as a sign that heaven and earth are inseparable, that both belong to Christ and are honoured by Christ.

But the material world is subject to decay and death. The body is subject to disease. We fear AIDS not least because it brings these realities home to us, graphically and inescapably. We fear the "bodiliness" of AIDS, the way it confronts us with our physical, mortal nature over which we do not have control despite miraculous medical advances. The human body is still wild. We have not yet tamed it to do our will: it becomes ill, it grows old, it dies; it is beautiful and strong, frail and fallible; it is breakable and finally, one day, it is broken.

Facing these realities, we cry out in our need for healing, for freedom from this bondage to decay. And in Jesus' ministry we find a pattern for our own embodiment. For there we see Christ incarnate, embracing the conditions of our own humanity (Phil. 2:6-8). Jesus serves wherever there is need. He shrinks from no situation, however horrifying or repulsive: not from the wounds of the lepers (Matt. 8:2-3), nor even from the stench of Lazarus, four days in the tomb (John 11:39). He befriends those who are condemned by uncleanness like the woman with the flow of blood (Mark 5:25-34) or who are cast out because of their ethnic identity or sexual behaviour like the woman at the well (John 4:7-30), or who are ostracized because of their fraudulent dealings like Zacchaeus (Luke 19:1-10). He accepts ministry from those deemed to have nothing to offer, like Mary who anointed him with ointment (John 12:1-8).

Jesus' deeds show us that, in the midst of the pain, brokenness and decay of our world, healing is yet possible, indeed *necessary*. Where there is no apparent hope, where death abounds, and against all odds, Jesus' act of service creates community and signifies life.

As the body of Christ, the church is called to such a ministry of service from within the suffering of the world. It can bear this task because it knows that, whatever its present condition may be, the material world is created by and dear to God. It is held within the love and care of Christ and it is destined for glory through the Spirit (Rom. 8:1-30). Because the things of this world are valuable and worthy of love and honour, the church will be slow to condemn even those things which seem in the eyes of the world to participate most irrevocably in the world's degradation and decay.

The church enacts this mystery of the material as a bearer of the divine each time it gathers about the table for that banquet at which Christ is meal and host and guest. Taking the things of the material world, it offers them up to God, signifying their true identity and home, and sending us forth in service to the world which God has made.

NOTES

[1] In Benedict Ward, ed., *Apophthegmata Patrum (The Wisdom of the Fathers)*, London, SLG Press, 1977, p.61.
[2] Quoted in the *Minutes* of the central committee, *loc. cit.*, p.135.
[3] St Basil, *Ascetic Works*, 2.1.
[4] Richard Holloway, in the introduction to *Who Needs Feminism? Male Responses to Sexism in the Church*, London, SPCK, 1991, pp.1-2.

CHAPTER 4

Ethical Perspectives

The HIV/AIDS pandemic confronts Christians and churches with many difficult ethical questions. How should churches respond to their own members who are living with or affected by HIV/AIDS? Should churches actively promote measures to limit the spread of HIV infection? How should resources for care, prevention and basic research be distributed? How can conditions favouring the spread of HIV/AIDS be corrected — and what do the churches have to say about such matters? What is the individual responsibility of Christians in this area? How can Christians and the churches decide about such matters?

The distinctive character of Christian ethical reflection

In approaching the challenge of HIV/AIDS, Christians are motivated by urgent imperatives passionately felt: to show Christ's love for the neighbour, to save lives, to work for reconciliation, to see that justice is done. Making decisions in this area, however, requires gathering the latest and most accurate information, wrestling with deeply sensitive issues and weighing differing and sometimes conflicting views and interests. That is to say: the passionate concern must energize and inform a process of *discernment*, which needs to be undergirded by Bible study, prayer and theological reflection.

Christians make ethical choices in accordance with certain principles, which follow from their understanding of the biblical witness and their faith convictions. These are stated in various ways by different Christians and Christian traditions, but they are likely to include the following points:

- because all human beings are created and beloved by God, Christians are called to treat every person as of infinite value;

- because Christ died to reconcile all to God, Christians are called to work for true reconciliation — which includes justice — among those alienated one from another;

- because we are "members one of another", being built up by the Spirit into one body, Christians are called to responsible life within community.

Applying these principles — the infinite value of each person, the gospel imperative for reconciliation, the call to responsible life within community — to the concrete challenges HIV/AIDS poses day by day to Christians and the churches involves gathering information about each specific problem, exploring all available options, weighing the benefits (and potential difficulties) of each and finally asking, "which of the possible courses of action best expresses Christ's love for all those concerned?"

This process of discernment is often difficult: the results of various courses of action may not be fully evident, none of the available options may be wholly satisfactory, the biblical mandate for some contemporary situations may not be clear, or Christians may disagree on how to apply a particular theological principle to a specific problem. This makes it all the more important that Christians and churches reflect on the ethical issues *together* rather than separately, that they respect and dialogue with views different from their own and that they work together to respond to the challenges posed by HIV/AIDS to both church and world.

Churches are expected to give both spiritual direction and moral guidance — not only within their own communities but also in the larger society — about issues raised by the HIV/AIDS pandemic. Thus in addition to their internal and ecumenical discussions, they should continue to play a responsible role in discussions of such issues in society as a whole, including more specialized considerations of biomedical ethics. Speaking from their own faith convictions they enrich the wider debate, in which they encounter those who appeal to general ethical principles such as the unconditional value of all persons, benevolence and justice.

Of the crucial contributions the churches have to make to this wider debate, two may be mentioned. First, because of their *commitment to truth*, the churches should emphasize the need for accurate information and for open discussion of the issues in the process of ethical decision-making. The process of discernment leaves no room for judgments based on superficial generalizations or stereotypes, on fear, or on incomplete or false information. It is essential to draw on medical and other expertise for an accurate factual understanding of the challenge of HIV/AIDS, though this is a background to — and not a substitute for — the process of ethical decision-making itself. The churches can do much to promote, both in their own lives and in the wider society, a climate of sensitive, factual and open exploration of the ethical issues posed by the pandemic.

Second, in accordance with their *emphasis on personal and communal responsibility*, the churches should promote conditions which support persons in making ethical choices. Speaking of personal responsibility implies a degree of personal freedom. This is directly related to the HIV/AIDS pandemic: it is well known that HIV spreads more freely when cultural and socio-economic factors make the exercise of personal and social responsibility difficult. Indeed, many persons today are so disempowered that they have lost the freedom to choose courses of action which are ethically and practically better. For example, women, even within marriage, may not have the power to insist on the practice of such effective preventive measures as abstinence, mutual fidelity and condom use.

The churches' ethical response to the issues raised by HIV/AIDS is inspired by the gospel. If this response is to make its strongest and widest witness and help as many persons as possible, it should commend itself not only to those within the church but also to reasonable people of good will in modern pluralistic and secularized societies.

To be convincing, this response will have to be *informed*. Entry into the ethical dialogue requires a comprehensive knowledge of basic ethical principles, a grasp of the personal and social dimensions of the problem, and clear scientific and technical information. A well-informed, transparent and verifiable ethical discussion and decision-making process on the part of the churches will surely meet with a ready response today. People in all societies have high expectations of receiving, through ethical considerations, answers to their burning questions and moral dilemmas. Churches in particular are looked to for moral guidance, and they have a unique opportunity to convey to the world a relevant message in a time of moral and political crisis.

This message should be a contribution to a peaceful and just co-existence of individuals and nations.

The churches' witness is hampered by the considerable disagreement within the Christian community on how to approach certain ethical issues, threatening the spirit of "unity in diversity" which characterizes the ecumenical movement. The challenges and possibilities are identified in the following statement from the Joint Working Group between the World Council of Churches and the Roman Catholic Church:

> Renewed expectations rise in and beyond the churches that religious communities can and should offer moral guidance in the public arena... Pressing personal and social moral issues, however, are prompting discord among Christians themselves and even threatening new divisions within and between churches... In a prayerful, non-threatening atmosphere, dialogue can locate more precisely where occur the agreements, disagreements and contradictions. And dialogue can affirm those shared convictions to which the churches should bear common witness to the world at large. Furthermore, the dialogue can discern how ethical beliefs and practices relate to that unity in moral life which is Christ's will. [1]

As the churches reflect on the meaning of the HIV/AIDS pandemic and look for solutions to the many problems it causes, they will inevitably engage in ethical discussion in the wider society. The following sections explore the relation between the perspectives and principles characteristic of this wider ethical reflection and the distinctive features of Christian ethical commitment.

Ethical perspectives and principles

Ethics is the systematic study of moral reasoning in theory and practice. It clarifies questions about right and wrong, but also demonstrates their complexity: most ethical theories, and many moral judgments, are contestable. Some norms, values or principles have found sufficiently wide agreement for codes of professional practice or laws to be based on them, but no ethical theory or decision-making method yields unequivocal conclusions which convince everybody. Too many different beliefs, philosophies, cultural backgrounds and life experiences influence our views of right and wrong. Nevertheless, meaningful and constructive frameworks developed by ethical reflection over the ages can be used to examine the facts and values in question, leading to a degree of consensus, or at least a mutual understanding of divergent views.

1. Ethical perspectives: two approaches

Ethical reflection asks about the "rightness" of particular actions. In the philosophical tradition, such reflection has proceeded from one of two starting points: either from the *norms* which are understood to govern human behaviour, or from the *consequences* which follow from that behaviour. A brief review of these two broad approaches — known as "deontology" and "consequentialism" (or "utilitarianism") respectively — will serve to introduce our discussion of specific forms of ethical reflection in the context of HIV/AIDS.

Deontology. The doctrine of duty, or "deontology", is characteristic of some of the oldest ethical systems in all cultures. It focuses on the "intrinsic" or given duties and values formulated as commandments and rules for human behaviour, which determine our actions. These are understood to be a matter of principle and to have, in themselves, their own undeniable justification.

The formulation and justification of these deontological values can originate from different perspectives. The Ten Commandments in the Old Testament (Ex. 20:1-17; Deut. 5:6-21), for example, are an ethical code based on divine revelation. The Golden Rule — "Do to others as you would have them do to you" (Luke 6:31) — is found in the New Testament and echoed in varied forms in many world religions; it serves as a general guideline for assessing human behaviour. Deontological philosophical reasoning — for example, Immanuel Kant's "supreme moral law" ("Act only on that maxim which you can, at the same time, will that it should become a universal law") — is intended to convince all reasonable people by its inherent logic. In sum, there are, according to this approach, moral rules and values which can be regarded as being universal and as forming the basis for principles and ideals to be translated into concrete moral actions.

Consequentialism (utilitarianism). Alternatively, consequentialism or utilitarianism claims that the question of right or wrong is decided by the consequences of an action. The moral quality of an action does not depend on the action itself, but on its "utility" in benefitting persons, that is, its effectiveness in promoting happiness or in achieving the "greatest good for the greatest number". Since this theory is based on only one moral principle, the principle of utility, there can be no conflicts between alternative principles of behaviour: to arrive at a decision about right and wrong, it is necessary to calculate net benefits and to balance alternative solutions, taking into consideration the resources available and the needs of the people concerned.

The supremacy of utility as a principle does not mean that just any type of action can be justified so long as it results in greater benefit for a person or group of persons. A particular version of this theory, called "rule utilitarianism", regards truth-telling, respect for life, keeping promises and so on as essential elements of the fabric of human life. These moral rules are to be observed because the overall benefit of keeping them is greater than that derived from neglecting them, even if disregarding them in individual cases might produce some benefit. The principle of utility, however, is still regarded as the supreme principle in the event that moral rules come into conflict with each other.

2. Ethical principles

These obviously broad and general *perspectives* on ethical reflection need to be supplemented by more concrete *principles* of ethical analysis, which can serve as guidelines for making ethical decisions in specific situations. In the area of health-care ethics today, the most widely used framework incorporates four principles: (1) respect for persons, (2) beneficence, (3) non-maleficence, and (4) justice. [2] Each of the four principles represents a prima-facie duty — that is, each is morally binding unless it conflicts with one of the others. But the framework does not provide a method for choosing between conflicting principles or determining the scope of their application (for example, regarding the first, there may be disagreement about who counts as a "person").

While these general principles may be used to analyze ethical issues and problems in many fields, it is especially helpful here to explore them in relation to medical ethics. Doctors, nurses and other health-care professionals urgently need ethical guidelines when treating patients and others affected by HIV/AIDS, testing new drugs or seeking personal and social measures to limit the spread of the disease;

and there has been intense ethical reflection within the health-care community on issues related to HIV/AIDS. This offers an important resource for Christian ethical reflection and can also an illustrate how the four principles could be applied in other areas (for example, to ethical problems arising in pastoral care and counselling for those affected by HIV/AIDS).

In medical ethics generally, and in ethics related to HIV/AIDS in particular, problems often arise which involve extremely complex and intrinsically ambiguous issues. Facing a choice between different notions of what is "right" and "wrong" in a specific situation, one can often find "conclusive" arguments to support several or perhaps all of the possible decisions. In itself this set of principles cannot resolve such situations; there might be mutually-exclusive decisions, each of which is supported by certain of the principles while violating others. This creates an ethical dilemma: often the question facing us is not *whether or not* to violate certain theories or principles, but which possible alternative violates them *more or less*.

But even if these principles cannot in themselves resolve ethical dilemmas, they do add an accessible ethical dimension to the international scientific vocabulary and provide a common language in which to address, analyze and discuss questions of cross-cultural concern. An additional advantage is that this framework can be employed by the two main schools of thought in philosophical ethics (deontology and consequentialism or utilitarianism) and accepted by adherents of many religious traditions. Even when those with different philosophical or religious views qualify the principles or their scope, the common core language remains "ecumenical". Moreover, these particular principles were originally identified by examining ethical codes and standards (especially of the health-care professions) which had been deeply influenced by Judaeo-Christian history.

Principle One: respect for persons
While many would agree that a person cannot or should not be considered as a distinct entity outside of relationships or community, the focus of the term in this principle is the human being capable of exercising a degree of autonomy, however limited. Autonomy is, literally, "self-rule" — the capacity to think, to make decisions and to act for oneself. It may be limited by immaturity, by lack of relevant information or by physical constraint. The capacity

for autonomy is a matter of degree, and is greater or less in different persons at different times. Ensuring maximum respect for the autonomy of people who are inarticulate, impaired or constrained may require special skills in listening or enabling, or in the political arena.

To exercise their autonomy, people need access to relevant information on which to base their decisions, as well as a degree of liberty which ensures that they make these decisions without undue coercion or manipulation.

Principles Two and Three: beneficence and non-maleficence

Beneficence is literally "doing good"; non-maleficence is "not doing harm". The first of these principles speaks of the duty to enhance the welfare of other people if one is in a position to do so. The second reflects what has been considered the most important moral principle for physicians since the time of Hippocrates: "Above all, do not harm." Together these two duties require physicians to produce net medical benefit with minimal harm. In order to determine what is in the best interests of a person who is temporarily or permanently unable to express his or her own autonomy, not only medical evidence but also the insights of other carers and friends may have to be taken into account.

Principle Four: justice

The principle of justice or fairness is more wide-ranging than the previous three, and thus may be appealed to if they are in conflict. While the principles of respect for persons and beneficence are concerned more (though not exclusively) with individual ethics, justice is more concerned with social ethics, with the treatment of persons in communities, with the question of right and wrong actions within and between communities, societies or nations.

Justice is especially concerned with the distribution of goods, services and resources. All human beings are presupposed to be of equal worth; and attributes like status, gender, wealth or merit do not justify inequalities. Not all inequalities are unfair: people have very different needs, and while those with equal needs should be treated equally, those with unequal needs should be treated unequally, that is, differently but within the claims of justice or fairness.

Justice is concerned with formulating criteria for resolving conflicts which arise between people because of widely differing conceptions of what people "deserve" or do not "deserve". These depend not only on a person's convictions, but also on his or her relative position within the local, national or global community. In the context of HIV/AIDS, justice is related both to questions about the distribution of scarce resources in health care and to the larger issues of poverty and economic constraints as contributing factors to the spread of HIV.

Christian and other ethical approaches in relation to the four principles

These principles are, as noted earlier, acceptable to the two main schools of thought in philosophical ethics. Respect for persons corresponds both to Kant's (deontological) imperative always to treat people as ends and not means and to John Stuart Mill's (utilitarian) requirement that everyone should be free to determine his or her own actions so long as these do not infringe on the autonomy of others. Both schools also accept beneficence and non-maleficence, although they may disagree on the scope of these principles, on how to work out their implications and on whether beneficence is an obligation for everyone or a praiseworthy virtue. Justice, too, is an agreed goal, though pursued by different strategies. For example, libertarian ethics leaves distributive justice largely to market forces, while egalitarian ethics demands that all people get the same share. Some theories restrict liberty in order to achieve a greater degree of justice; others (for example, Rawls's contract theory) give liberty priority over equality — but only if allowing inequalities is actually to the benefit of the least advantaged. [3]

Most other contemporary approaches to medical ethics are compatible with and complementary to the four-principles approach. *Case-based* methods, which attempt to revive the best methods of traditional casuistry, relate concrete examples to agreed principles. *Narrative or story-telling ethics* (which resembles the Christian method of telling parables) can also relate constructively to the four principles. *Virtue ethics*, which emphasizes that the right choices are most likely to be made by "good" people, focuses on other aspects of the moral spectrum which need to be taken into account. The same is true of *care* approaches, which emphasize context, relationships, the particular persons and circumstances involved and compassion.

The only serious effort to replace the four principles is the *common morality* approach. This offers a deductive method which, it is claimed, can find the correct answers to specific ethical questions. But there are two main difficulties with this: (1) the exclusive claims it makes for its own interpretations of "rationality" and "common morality" are contestable; (2) the proposed deductive system of decision-making is not only very complicated, but also depends on getting people to agree about a series of more or less abstract value judgments before they can reach the correct concrete judgment about the ethical question in hand.

Turning again to Christian ethics, another approach — which would also be relevant for general ethical behaviour — is proposed by H. Richard Niebuhr, who describes ethics-in-a-relationship as a "dialogue of responsibility". The two ethical questions Niebuhr discerns are "What is going on in this situation?" (in other words, one must be well-informed) and "What is the fitting thing to do?" (that is, the action which best fits the dialogue at this point and allows it to continue). Because the "fitting" action will depend on particular circumstances, it can never be specified in the abstract or in advance. Thus responsible discernment is required of those involved in making the necessary ethical choices.[4]

Christian ethics derives from theological reflection on Scripture and the churches' response to revelation. Rather than putting forward a single comprehensive ethical theory, it embraces principles and values drawn from historical and personal Christian experience and, for some, from natural law. It is deontological in seeing obedience to God's living Word as the supreme rule for conscience and community. But its incarnational and eschatological orientation regards as God-given the human freedom to respond to the complexity and ambiguities of ordinary moral experience — an opportunity to grow, through mutual forgiveness, in grace and understanding.

The WCC-Roman Catholic Joint Working Group text cited above also mentions other Christian resources, in addition to the Bible, for moral reflection. These include the liturgy, traditional moral teaching, catechisms and sermons, time-honoured pastoral practices, wisdom distilled from past and present experience, and the arts of reflection and spiritual discernment. Given the complex social, scientific and technical issues posed by HIV/AIDS in the modern context, it is important to recognize that

> the biblical vision by itself does not provide Christians with all the clear moral principles and practical norms they need. Nor do the Scriptures resolve every ethical case...
>
> Nevertheless, there is a general consensus that by prayerfully studying the Scriptures and the developing traditions of biblical interpretations, by reflecting on human experiences, and by sharing insights within a

community, Christians can reach reasonable judgments and decisions in many cases of ethical conduct.[5]

These judgments and decisions of Christian ethics are in harmony with the four principles of bioethics as described above. But they also go beyond them, since they derive from notions of relationship. God relates to all creation, both its human and non-human aspects, which in turn are in relation with each other. Thus a principle such as the autonomy of persons may be found in the unconditional value of all creatures (Matt. 10:29-30), or in Paul's respect for the conscience of the Gentiles (Rom. 2:4). Yet as God not only respected the freedom of the world but also loved it (John 3:16), so Christians should not only respect the autonomy of others, but ought to love their neighbours also.

For Christians, beneficence is a basic duty, but Christian ethics goes beyond the moral rule of beneficence which is required of everyone at all times. Because it comes within the command to "love your neighbour as yourself" (Matt. 22:39; Mark 12:31; Luke 10:25-28), beneficence, wherever possible, includes *benevolence* (or good-will). Jesus taught as a characteristic feature of the values of the kingdom of God not only doing what is required by law but doing more out of love: going also "the second mile" (Matt. 5:41).[6]

While we may not find a comprehensive theory of distributive justice in the Bible, "justice" is an important and frequently-used biblical concept. It is a relational concept asserting the inescapable interrelatedness of all things. Equality is again supported by the story of creation itself, and the Bible reminds us repeatedly that our first and foremost concern has to be those who are in greatest need. In Old Testament terms, those in greatest need were the widows, orphans and strangers, towards whom all Israelites had special obligations. In the New Testament it is the poor, despised and marginalized who first understand the message of the kingdom of God, and Jesus Christ meets us in the least of his brothers and sisters. It must be remembered that all these groups are exactly those who are nowadays most affected by HIV/AIDS.

Ethics applied to some issues raised by HIV/AIDS

The bioethical problems raised by HIV/AIDS are often complex and ambiguous, and the arguments for one choice or another are seldom if ever conclusive. Yet practical decision-making is urgently required. The people involved in this decision-making are of all faiths or none, and differentiating among the possible solutions requires sound facts and technical information. In order to go beyond rhetoric, therefore, Christian ethical insights in this realm must first be expressed in a language that can be understood by all informed people of good will, then translated into meaningful action. The application of the four principles to the particular problems and questions posed by HIV/AIDS can be regarded as a touchstone for the validity and the soundness of the arguments. In what follows we shall look more closely at nine of these issues.

1. Discrimination

Discrimination against people living with HIV/AIDS unfortunately occurs in all societies and communities, and has become an important obstacle to effective means against the further spread of the pandemic. Discrimination makes the whole community — both those who discriminate and those discriminated against — more vulnerable to the spread of HIV. In a situation of stigmatization, prejudice and gossip, both groups are less likely to accept the presence of HIV in the community and to co-operate in the prevention of the factors which lead to increased vulnerability to HIV. Resistance to discrimination against people affected by HIV is thus an integral part of prevention.

All the ethical principles require that no one be discriminated against because of attributes such as race, gender, religion or being affected by a particular disease. The principles of beneficence and non-maleficence are clearly violated in the case of discrimination, since it causes considerable harm not only to those who are discriminated against but also, eventually, to those who discriminate. Again, justice demands that people be treated equally and fairly so that they receive the care and attention they need.

2. Confidentiality

Confidentiality means that information which persons wish to keep to themselves or share only with a person they trust (such as a doctor or counsellor) in fact remains secret. Such a relationship of mutual trust is protected by special obligations. Confidentiality of personal health information is implied by the principle of respect for persons, and required by traditional medical ethics. Lack of privacy inhibits responsible decision-making.

This fact is particularly important in relation to sensitive information such as a person's HIV serostatus, ways of infection or symptoms of AIDS. By maintaining confidentiality and trust, doctors or counsellors may have an opportunity to influence behaviour, thereby reducing the risk of the transmission of HIV infection to others; whereas disrespect for the principle of confidentiality may lead people infected with HIV to fear that their status could be disclosed to others, thus driving them underground and impairing the positive opportunities of the doctor-patient relationship.

However, there may be situations of conflicting principles, in which someone discloses his or her HIV serostatus to a doctor or counsellor but refuses to reveal it to others who are at risk through mutual relationships. The dilemma of the doctor or counsellor (which is heightened if he or she is caring for both partners) is whether to respect the first client's autonomy or to breach confidentiality in order to avoid potentially fatal harm to the partner. The principle of autonomy demands strict confidentiality and prohibits the disclosure of this information to a third party. The principles of beneficence and non-maleficence demand that the life of persons be protected by providing them information they need to avoid a serious infection. But that in turn may make it less likely that such information will be confined to doctors or counsellors in the future. So in this particular case respecting the duty of non-maleficence may have long-term consequences which are medically more harmful than beneficial.

Both principles have to be balanced, and each particular case has to be treated with extreme care and sensitivity throughout the process of ethical decision-making. Every attempt must be made to help the client to disclose the information to his or her partner voluntarily. Only when this fails utterly may the doctor or counsellor consider overriding the principle of confidentiality, always on a strict need-to-know basis. [7]

Decisions of this kind are agonizing for those who have to make them. In fact, they are relatively rare, since a normally trustful doctor- or counsellor-patient relationship will almost always be able to avoid steps which might violate confidentiality. Much more common is the need to ensure that confidentiality is not breached inadvertently or carelessly.

3. Sex, AIDS and health education

In some cultural environments, people refuse to talk about sex, AIDS and aspects of sexual health. Many people of good will fear that more open talk about sex and sex education will result in a corresponding increase of promiscuous behaviour. Clearly the church has a moral responsibility to minimize communal and personal vulnerability to conditions in which sexually transmitted disease might spread, and education is a major contribution towards this goal (see above, pp.10-13).

In spite of understandable reservations, research has revealed that education about sex, AIDS and health in general, particularly with children and young people, does not result in increased sexual activity.[8] The responsibility of the church in facilitating sound, well-resourced education is thus evident.

Equipping people, particularly children and youth, with the ability to make sound moral decisions is the most effective way of achieving responsible moral behaviour. But education is more than knowledge. Increasing the number of facts people know will not necessarily turn them into well-equipped decision-makers. Effective education is responsive to the cultural context into which information is introduced, and involves the mutual participation of educators and students (see above, p.11).

4. Condoms

The promotion and use of the condom, a simple technical device to prevent the exchange of body fluids during sexual intercourse, has raised considerable concern among Christians and churches. Some have perceived this as contradicting the teaching that abstinence from or mutual fidelity within sexual relationships is the safest method of HIV prevention (see above, p.11). Others have also raised questions about the safety and efficacy of condoms, although a carefully designed study cited by the World Health Organization offers clear scientific evidence that the condom is a safe and effective means of protection from sexually transmitted diseases.

Condom breakage and slippage has been analyzed, both through studies in which participants have been surveyed about their condom use and through studies in which participants have been given condoms and asked to report on various aspects of their use. One US consumer survey of almost 3300 people reported condom breakage rates of less than one percent.

Laboratory studies have also been carried out to assess leakage of a variety of micro-organisms, including HIV. These studies have demonstrated the ability of intact latex membranes to prevent the passing of HIV, herpes and hepatitis B viruses, cytomegalovirus and chlamydia trachomatis, even after mechanical stimulation.

Conclusion of the study: Condoms, when used consistently and correctly, are highly effective at reducing the risk of infection from HIV and other sexually transmitted diseases. Therefore, efforts focused on improving condom quality, availability and use represent a critical aspect of public health strategies to contain these diseases.

"A Response to Recent Questions about Latex Condom Effectiveness in Preventing Sexual Transmission of the AIDS Virus", prepared by the Program for Appropriate Technology in Health (PATH), Seattle, USA, January 1994

Ethical questions are raised in connection with the effects on behaviour of the use and promotion of condoms. Some would argue that the promotion of condom use might increase promiscuous sexual behaviour; while others contend that sexual behaviour is largely determined by other factors, and that what condoms affect is not the frequency of sexual intercourse but the unwanted consequences of this behaviour, that is, the sexual transmission of diseases.

So far, no conclusive studies have shown that the promotion and use of condoms influence promiscuous sexual behaviour. But the implications of the conflicting arguments here will be influenced by the ethical principles applied. For example, there might be a conflict between the desire to protect people's moral integrity by reducing incentives for sexual promiscuity and the desire to protect human life by averting a potentially lethal infection.

The principle of respect for persons favours self-determination, which would require promoting access both to information about protection from infection and to the protective device itself. On this view, even if condoms also have negative effects, it would be paternalistic to withhold from people the information they need in order to decide for themselves whether to use them.

If the promotion of condoms could reduce the risk of HIV transmission, the principles of beneficence and of non-maleficence would imply a moral obligation to save lives by enabling people to protect themselves. The principle of justice would demand that all those who need a protective method have access to it — and not only those who live in societies where these methods are freely available or who have the ability to pay.

Because of these arguments many Christian health professionals and counsellors have decided, on the grounds of pastoral responsibility and after careful consideration, to provide their clients with condoms when specifically requested. This is done without claiming that condom use is or should be the only answer to the question of HIV prevention. Condoms are only one of a range of methods to prevent HIV transmission. The primary aim must be to change behaviour and social conditions in a way which puts people at a lower risk of coming into contact with the virus. All choices have to be presented to the people concerned, and every effort must be made to empower them to make responsible decisions for their own lives, based on the options available according to current knowledge and experience.

After careful consideration of the ethical questions and of the technical details, the following conclusion was drawn: *Without blessing or encouraging promiscuity, we recognize the reality of human sexual relationships and practice and of the existence of HIV in the world. Scientific evidence has demonstrated that education on positive measures of prevention and the provision and use of condoms help to prevent transmission of the virus and the consequent suffering and death for many of those infected. Should not the churches, in the light of these facts, recognize the use of condoms as a method of prevention of HIV?*

5. Clean needles for people addicted to injectable drugs

Among people addicted to injectable drugs the sharing of needles and syringes is one of the principal ways of HIV transmission. Providing clean needles and syringes to those who use these devices is thus a method to prevent unintended HIV transmission caused by unsterile instruments. As a technique, this does not pose any ethical problem. But since the use of certain injectable drugs, such as heroin, is illegal in many countries, and since societies try to discourage their use, the provision of the means to inject these drugs may be questioned ethically.[9]

Intervention programmes for drug addicts have used various methods of HIV prevention, including the introduction of needle-exchange schemes. Evaluations of comprehensive programmes in several cities have shown that the combination of these methods has been effective in regard to HIV prevention without increasing the use of drugs.[10] There is thus a strong moral obligation, based on all four of the principles, to apply these methods, since they have the potential to save lives.

Again it should be remembered that needle-exchange programmes and other interventions are only one method for reducing the many risks and threats to human life posed by the use of narcotic drugs. The best way, of course, of reducing HIV transmission through infected needles would be the primary prevention of drug use itself. All programmes, irrespective of their methods, should be culturally acceptable, accessible and based on voluntary participation.

After careful consideration of the ethical questions and of the technical details the following conclusion was drawn: *Without blessing or encouraging the use of narcotic, intravenously applied drugs, we recognize the reality of human addiction to these drugs and the practice of sharing needles for the application of these drugs, which carries a high risk of HIV transmission. Studies on established programmes have demonstrated that education and the provision of clean needles help to reduce the risk of viral transmission and the consequent suffering and death for many of those infected by this way. Should not the churches, in the light of these facts, recognize the need for appropriate education and for the provision with clean needles for all those who are addicted to injectable drugs?*

6. HIV testing

Respect for persons requires that no one should be forced to undergo a diagnostic or therapeutic procedure affecting his or her future without all the information needed to make an independent and informed decision about whether or not the procedure should be performed. Explicit consent is not required for all laboratory tests. For routine investigations which carry no particular risk and are necessary for treatment, a patient's general consent or evident wish to be treated is sufficient. But the HIV test is different from such routine investigations, not only because the condition diagnosed is still incurable, but also because of its personal, social and economic consequences for the people concerned, who will face discrimination and stigmatization once their infection is made public.

Therefore HIV testing should be done only if informed consent of the person concerned has been obtained without any form of coercion or persuasion, and if appropriate pre- and post-test counselling is provided. This implies that compulsory HIV testing for any purpose — including testing for admission to jobs, education, entry into countries, medical treatment — is to be regarded as unethical. Moreover, testing before marriage, if recommended, must be voluntary on the part of both partners.

Voluntary testing, in combination with counselling and under strict observance of confidentiality, is often requested by people who would like to know their HIV-serostatus to help them to make responsible decisions about their future life. This service should be made available wherever possible.

A potential conflict could arise between the individual rights of a person infected with HIV and the rights of a society wishing to protect a large number of its members by control mechanisms which restrict those individual rights (see below, pp. 73-74). Arguments of utility have been used during some past epidemics to justify overriding the individual's rights to informed consent or to confidentiality in favour of the rights of the majority. In practice, however, these extreme measures are neither necessary nor useful in the case of HIV infection. Taking into consideration the experience after the first decade of the HIV pandemic, there is now international agreement that the best way of prevention is providing information and seeking voluntary co-operation — not coercion or compulsory testing.

7. Research

Several ethical problems are posed by research related to HIV/ AIDS, including research on human subjects in the development of new drugs, access to experimental drugs by desperately ill patients and guidelines for the conduct of vaccine development and trials.

International codes and guidelines regulate ethical preconditions for all research studies involving human subjects. The Nuremberg Code (1947), the Declaration of Helsinki of the World Medical Association (1975) and the International Guidelines for Ethics and Epidemiology of the Council for International Organizations of Medical Sciences (CIOMS) (1990) protect the rights of those who take part in any form of trial in the search for new treatments or vaccines. These codes clearly state that persons should only be invited to participate voluntarily, and after informed consent has been given, in trials which are scientifically worthwhile and in which the risks to subjects have been minimized.

Trials related to HIV/AIDS are no exception to this, but problems arise when taking part is the only hope desperately ill patients have for receiving any potentially effective treatment. The principle of non-maleficence obliges researchers to increase only slowly and in careful stages the number of persons receiving an experimental therapy, as evidence accumulates of its effectiveness and of the absence of harmful side-effects. This may conflict with the autonomy of patients who wish to decide for themselves whether or not to risk the side-effects of a potentially beneficial therapy. Yet if the wishes of too many such patients are granted, the trial may be invalidated, an unproven or even harmful drug promoted and research on promising alternatives delayed — all to the detriment of future patients. Such conflicts can be overcome only by the ethical sensitivity, forbearance and mutual understanding of researchers and patients alike.

Research on experimental therapies may require that some subjects receive, for purposes of comparison, not the therapy itself, but a placebo — something ineffectual and harmless which however looks like the actual therapy. The ethical problems of this are intensified in HIV vaccine trials. Research into the effectiveness of an experimental vaccine may require the subjects to be at continuing risk if the trials are to demonstrate whether a potential vaccine is effective or not. Here the ethical problem is compounded by the possibility that participation may create a false sense of security and also that the risk could be reduced by health education.

In addition to these concerns following from the principle of non-maleficence, there are considerations of justice, which arise when those recruited are too poor or too ill-informed to decline to participate. At the very least, justice requires that risks and benefits in the development, production and distribution of potential therapies and vaccines are shared globally, without placing vulnerable groups or countries at a disadvantage.

8. Allocation of resources

The just allocation of resources is a major presupposition for an adequate care of people living with HIV/AIDS and for effective prevention of the spread of the infection. This applies to all levels of social and economic structures.

At the community level, personal, financial, emotional and spiritual resources must be mobilized to achieve the full participation of persons living with AIDS in the life of the community, and to give them the care required for their physical and emotional well-being. At the national level HIV/AIDS has to receive the degree of attention, support from leaders in society and government and mobilization of resources which is warranted by the significance of the problem, in terms both of the human suffering involved and the social and economic implications of the pandemic for the country. Globally, the international community has to ensure that adequate measures are taken for the fight against a worldwide pandemic, which affects all regions and continents.

So far, the distribution of resources for the treatment and care of AIDS patients and the prevention of HIV transmission has been extremely unequal: although more than 80 percent of all HIV infections occur in less-affluent countries, they receive only a small portion of the international resources spent on HIV/AIDS.[11] This raises serious questions of distributive justice. Justice requires the most care for those in greatest need. This means, in practice, that available resources should be redistributed, giving all countries a fair share and enabling them to establish programmes adapted to their local situations. From a short-term political and economic perspective, this may seem unrealistic. But the aims of such an action — to reduce both the burden on those directly affected and the further spread of the infection — is consonant with the global common good at a time when, economically as well as epidemiologically, world populations are becoming increasingly interdependent.

9. *The duties of health professionals to treat persons living with AIDS*

Unfortunately, there are reports of people living with HIV/AIDS being refused entry to health-care institutions — including those of the churches — and of being refused by individual health-care professionals whom they have approached for treatment, help or advice. Neither ethically nor historically can these attitudes be justified. Access to health care is a *right* for all persons, including those infected with HIV. There are no medical or moral grounds for any restriction of this right.

Some health professionals have referred to the increased risk of contracting HIV which might arise from treating persons living with AIDS. This concern is not supported by the studies so far conducted on the occupational risks of health professionals. Very few health professionals who are HIV-positive can be proven to have contracted the infection though actions related to their professional duties.

Given proper observation of normal precautions, the risk of acquiring the infection occupationally is very small. Statistically, a needle prick with HIV-infected blood will lead to an infection in only three cases in a thousand. [12] Consequently the international bodies regulating professional conduct have so far insisted that people infected with HIV should be treated in the same way as other patients; and the refusal of treatment would be considered as a gross violation of the rules of professional conduct. This view would be supported by all four of the principles of bioethics.

NOTES

[1] "The Ecumenical Dialogue on Moral Issues: Potential Sources of Common Witness or of Divisions. A Study Document of the Joint Working Group of the Roman Catholic Church and the World Council of Churches," I.2-4, *The Ecumenical Review*, Vol. 48, no. 2, April 1996, pp.144f.

[2] See Tom Beauchamp and James Childress, *Principles of Biomedical Ethics*, 4th ed., New York, Oxford UP, 1994; Ranaan Gillon, *Principles of Health Care Ethics*, Chichester, UK, John Wiley & Sons, 1994.

[3] John Rawls, *A Theory of Justice*, New York, Oxford UP, 1972, p.302.

[4] See H. Richard Niebuhr, *The Responsible Self: An Essay in Christian Moral Philosophy*, New York, Harper & Row, 1963.

[5] "The Ecumenical Dialogue on Moral Issues", III.1, *loc. cit.*, p.147.

[6] John Habgood, "An Anglican View of the Four Principles," in Gillon, *op. cit.*, pp.55-64.

[7] Kenneth Boyd, "HIV Infection and AIDS: The Ethics of Medical Confidentiality", *Journal of Medical Ethics*, Vol. 18, 1992, pp.173-79.

[8] Results of the Research Study "Does Sex Education Lead to Earlier or Increased Sexual Activity in Youth?", by M. Baldo, P. Aggleton and G. Slutkin of the WHO, as presented at the IXth International AIDS Conference, Berlin, June 1993, documentation no. PO-D 02-344.

[9] M. O'Brien, "Needle Exchange Programs: Ethical and Policy Issues", *AIDS & Public Policy Journal*, Vol. 4, no. 2, 1989, pp.75-82.

[10] Erik von Ameijden et al., "Interventions among Injecting Drug Users: Do They Work?", in *AIDS*, Vol. 9 (suppl. A), 1995, S75-S84.

[11] Cf. "Vaccine Briefing", *Global AIDS News* (World Health Organization), no. 2, 1994, p.5.

[12] D. K. Henderson, et al., "Risk for Occupational Transmission of HIV-1 Associated with Clinical Exposures", in *Ann. Int. Med.*, Vol. 113, 1990, 740-46.

CHAPTER 5

Human Rights, Responsibilities and HIV/AIDS

Human rights have been identified and defended from various philosophical, religious and political perspectives, including individual liberal rights theory, natural law and moral theology, and theories of economic and social justice. Internationally recognized human rights have been drawn together and protected by such instruments as the Universal Declaration of Human Rights (1948) and the twin United Nations covenants — ratified by most governments — on economic, social and cultural rights, and on civil and political rights.

Over the last three decades the World Council of Churches has been actively involved in human rights standard-setting, promotion and protection. The last decade has witnessed a significant development of international norms and standards regarding people who are discriminated against on grounds of race, gender, ethnicity and religion. There are other kinds of discrimination as well, including that which arises out of lack of awareness and fear. Discrimination against people living with HIV/AIDS falls into this category. Such people are often denied their fundamental right to security, freedom of association, freedom of movement and adequate health care.

The violation of human rights in relation to HIV/AIDS is widespread. The pandemic spotlights many formerly unrecognized inequalities and prejudices in our societies and reinforces long-term disparities. People living with HIV/AIDS face isolation and discrimination in virtually all societies and cultures. Their physical symptoms are compounded by the psychological impacts associated with HIV/AIDS. The illness and death resulting from HIV/AIDS is frequently suffered in loneliness and abandonment, as people with AIDS are often isolated and even abused. People who find themselves infected with HIV suffer the loss of their own future, whether by losing the

The attainment of a just and humane society requires that all individuals and organizations both respect human rights and dignity and observe those principles of humanity which reflect universal human values shared by religions and cultures throughout the world.

Respect for the rights to life and to the highest attainable standard of health and for the principle of non-discrimination requires states to ensure that all sectors of society receive appropriate information and education on HIV and AIDS, and that particular attention is paid to reaching people in remote locations and members of disadvantaged groups.

From the "Declaration and Charter on HIV and AIDS"
of Rights and Humanity, the International Movement
for the Promotion and Realization of Human Rights
and Responsibilities, London

opportunity to have a family, or being deprived of chances for meaningful work, or losing other basic human rights.

Definitions, obligations and limitations

This study has worked with a basic understanding of human rights as all rights necessary for integrity, survival, growth and dignity in relation to the physical, spiritual and social being. Human rights is thus not only about individual liberty, but also about economic and social justice, and the relationship between individual, community and the state.

The source of human rights is the recognition of the equal worth and dignity of all human beings. Affirming human rights is not just a

HIV antibody testing must occur with free and informed consent, except in the case of unlinked, anonymous epidemiological screening programmes.

Segregation, isolation or quarantine of persons in prisons, schools, hospitals or elsewhere merely on the grounds of AIDS or HIV is unacceptable.

From "The AIDS Charter", published by the
AIDS Consortium, Centre for Applied Legal Studies,
University of Witwatersrand, South Africa

matter of political activism; it is a worldview which has to do with how we perceive ourselves as human beings (whether as equals or not), how we relate to each other and our communities (whether in aggressive competition and prejudice or in love and mutual respect) and the role of leadership (whether paternalistic and dominating or aiming at empowerment and facilitating of autonomy).

In the context of HIV/AIDS, there is a strong public health rationale for respect of human rights. Such rights impose the moral and legal imperative to ensure that everyone's equal worth and dignity is fully respected, without discrimination.

There are of course different interpretations of and approaches to human rights. This is evident in the arguments for and against the "universality" of human rights — the idea that everyone everywhere is entitled to the same fundamental human rights regardless of cultural, political or religious differences. Those who argue in favour of universality say that all human beings share similar basic needs and at least some core human values, from which universal norms for human rights can be developed. Others would contend that, in the light of the different cultural characteristics and distinct values of societies, no single value system can be regarded as having global application. Some would even call human rights a "Western" notion being imposed on them against their will, though at the same time many people from the countries or communities where this argument is made are risking their lives to uphold these very rights — which they consider fundamental to their own cultures and faiths.

Despite these different interpretations, the dignity and equality of human beings have become accepted values. An important aspect of this is striking the proper balance between the rights of one individual and those of another individual or of the community. This may require limitations of the exercise of rights. Such limitations need to be provided for by law and strictly justified; they must not be arbitrary.

From the above, one may conclude that each right will have a corresponding duty. For example, because the exercise of one's own rights takes place within a social context, one is constrained to respect the rights (and, according to some, to help to meet the needs) of others. Rights involve also responsibilities, but the relationship between the two is complex, and the latter are often not discussed out of a fear that such discussion might compromise the principle of the

> The duty of human solidarity requires everyone to cooperate in efforts to prevent and alleviate human suffering and strive against injustice. With respect to the protection of public health, international human rights jurisprudence and public health law and practice confirm that public health measures which restrict individual rights and liberties are justifiable only to the extent that they are:
>
> - provided for by a specific law,
>
> - strictly required for the protection of public health,
>
> - strictly proportional to the benefit to be gained from the policy or restrictive measure,
>
> - represent the least intrusive and restrictive method of achieving the desired end, and
>
> - not arbitrarily directed against a particular individual, group or section of society.
>
> *From the "Declaration and Charter on HIV and AIDS"*
> *of Rights and Humanity, London*

inalienability of human rights — the conviction that individuals remain entitled to such rights even if they fail to comply with their responsibilities.

The individual and the community

The complex relationship between rights and duties is confirmed by the status of human beings as created in the image of God. The Bible, rather than referring to "rights", speaks about duties to God within the covenant; this is in order to safeguard others from abuses and to give all people an equal possibility to benefit. God is described as *love*; and human beings, created in God's image, are therefore called and given the possibility to reflect that reality. The image of God is an inclusive description of the human family, not a cause for human pride. In light of this, humanity's very existence as love and *koinonia* should be approached according to the principles of relationships with others, including the natural world. Such an approach will in fact result in implementing the idea of human rights and duties.

For this reason, human rights also has to do with economic and social, environmental and ecological justice, and with the relationship between the individual, community and government. In saying this, however, it is important to be clear about the community's interests — and to identify who determines the nature of these. What is often put forward as *the* interest of the community may in fact be based on the selfish, individual interests of dominant "representatives" of the community.

In authentic *koinonia*, rights and duties are considered in harmony. The "individual", as usually described, does not prevail over the communitarian, but neither does the communitarian suppress the individual. From this theological perspective, the very idea of human rights can be looked at only in the light of life *in* community rather than *against* community.

There is consequently no necessary conflict between the rights of the person and the interests of the community. Human rights should be a tool for the empowerment of both persons and communities, in order to restore their dignity and enhance the quality of life.

Human rights vis-a-vis AIDS

The question of human rights in relation to HIV/AIDS is of course closely related to many of the ethical issues considered in the previous chapter; and this section, which focuses in particular on issues of justice, should be read in connection with that material.

1. Denial of human rights as a cause of vulnerability to HIV

At one point or another, all people affected by HIV and AIDS have their rights violated. But there is also growing evidence that people whose fundamental human rights are denied and who are economically or socially marginalized are especially vulnerable to the risk of HIV infection. AIDS follows the fault lines of our societies. Street children, those living in poverty, prisoners, commercial sex workers, drug-dependent persons, indigenous people and ethnic minorities are all at particular risk, and often show disproportionately high infection rates compared to the rest of their societies.

We have seen earlier (pp.13-18) that women are particularly vulnerable as a result of their disadvantaged economic, social and legal status. Lack of education, employment opportunities, independent income and adequate access to health-care facilities and treatment for sexually transmitted diseases all heighten the risk of HIV infection, as does lack of assertiveness in sexual matters.

A related and growing concern is violence against children. There has been an alarming rise in sex tourism, increasingly directed at partners who are children. And it is precisely in an effort to escape HIV infection that some men in both the North and the South abuse children and youth in an effort to escape infection.

2. The public health response

Protection of the right to life clearly requires states to take effective public health measures to control the spread of contagious disease. On this ground some people have suggested that it is permissible in the public interest to limit an individual's rights to liberty solely on the grounds of his or her HIV status. Fear and public ignorance surrounding AIDS have frequently led to public pressure for and even introduction of draconian policies to control the spread of HIV. Some AIDS laws and policies which have been introduced clearly violate fundamental human rights and ethical principles. In fact, there is no public health justification for limiting the individual liberty of persons living with AIDS, since HIV cannot be transferred through normal social contact.

3. Discrimination against people with HIV/AIDS or presumed to be at risk of infection

Perhaps the most widespread human rights abuses in the context of the AIDS pandemic are the discrimination and social stigma suffered by people with HIV/AIDS, their families and associates, and people considered to be at risk of infection, such as gay persons, prostitutes and drug users.

Sofia Gruskin speaks of the AIDS pandemic as sparking a new type of hate crime: "attacks on people because of an illness... AIDS-specific violence is just that: it generally involves reference to the disease. For some people, the fear of AIDS has provided a powerful, if misguided, rationalization for attacks on traditionally stigmatized groups, particularly gay men and female sex workers."[1]

The restoration of dignity

As indicated in the chapter on theological perspectives above (pp.43-44), any violation of human rights is contrary to Christian belief. Unfortunately, the reaction of many Christians and church members to HIV/AIDS has hardly been different from that of society in general — and sometimes has been even worse.

The HIV/AIDS pandemic calls attention to the importance of local heritage and tradition, as well as people-based knowledge and community processes. The challenge of the current situation is to recover and to reshape these crucial realities.

As they implement human rights while pursuing economic and social development, it is particularly important that communities participate in the light of their own experiences and values. The participation of people within the community is crucial. Because knowledge about human rights has implications for holding and using power, such knowledge should be available as a tool for the entire community. Similarly, the development and extension of human rights is something in which the entire community should be closely involved. The result should be a struggle for the holistic understanding and practice of human rights — a struggle in which the church plays an active role.

In the Participatory Action Research project in Kagoma, Uganda, the community started to discuss and address the issues of inequality and human rights within their local experience of HIV/AIDS. Through focus group discussions in the community, people realized that the underprivileged status of women was a problem for the whole community. Girls were deprived rights for education, which in turn made them vulnerable to sexual and economic exploitation, which could make them HIV-infected. Promoting education for girls was identified as a way of reducing the infection rate in that place. This was combined with enforcement of sanctions against rape. The groups also started to discuss traditional male-female roles and division of labour in the community, in order to propose changes and strategies to improve co-operation.

From the 1993 report Participatory Action Research on AIDS and the Community as a Source of Care and Healing, *co-published by the WCC, Christian Medical Board of Tanzania, Uganda Protestant Medical Bureau and Eglise du Christ au Zaïre*

Such a holistic view of human rights has not always been incorporated into people's understanding. In many struggles against injustice and oppression, people have been animated by secular understandings of human rights. Even people in the churches have fought for justice through agencies outside their churches.

The reality of HIV/AIDS existing in the individual, the community and the church creates a fresh opportunity for the church to *be with* its people — to leave the church buildings and to go and suffer with its people where they live. It is an opportunity for the church to reclaim as its own the struggle for the restoration of human rights.

The challenge to the church is: what is the extent of its role in advocating and protecting human rights in the context of HIV and AIDS? Some of the specific dimensions of that challenge are:

- to recognize that human rights are based on the equal worth and dignity of every human being;
- to consider that each individual and organ of society is under an obligation to respect the rights and dignity of others, to avoid harm and to act in compassion, tolerance and mutual solidarity; and that each has positive duties for the achievement of human well-being;
- to view human beings as whole — as physical, mental, psychological, spiritual and social beings. Such an approach requires recognition of the need of individuals to *belong* — to weave homes and communities. Thus the concept of community is an important element within an holistic understanding of human rights.

NOTE

[1] Sofia Gruskin, "HIV/AIDS-Related Violence", in *A Global Report: AIDS in the World*, pp.562f., Box 13.4.

CHAPTER 6

Pastoral Care and Healing Community

The church as a healing community

The church, by its very nature as the body of Christ, calls its members to become healing communities. Despite the extent and complexity of the problems raised by HIV/AIDS, the churches can make an effective healing witness towards those affected. The experience of love, acceptance and support within a community where God's love is made manifest can be a powerful healing force. This means that the church should not — as was often the case when AIDS was first recognized in the gay community — exclude, stigmatize and blame persons on the basis of behaviour which many local congregations and churches judge to be unacceptable.

It is important to acknowledge that the church is a communion of one body with many members, each distinct:

> But God has so arranged the body, giving the greater honour to the inferior member, that there may be no dissension within the body, but the members may have the same care for one another. If one member suffers, all suffer together with it; if one member is honoured, all rejoice together with it. Now you are the Body of Christ and individually members of it (1 Cor. 12:24b-27).

When the church properly responds to people living with HIV/AIDS, both ministering to them and learning from their suffering, its relationship to them will indeed make a difference, and thus become growth-producing. And if through this relationship — out of fidelity to others who are suffering and because of the significance of those who suffer — we are again pushed back on ourselves, it is because in the gospels we are *required* to love: this is a demand, a requirement, not an option.

Two months after the federal Centre for Disease Control's (CDC) 1981 report of the first cases of an illness to become known as AIDS, eighty men alarmed by the report gathered in New York writer Larry Kramer's apartment to hear a doctor speak about "gay cancer". Passing the hat, the men contributed $6635 for biomedical research. Six months later, this fund-raising group became Gay Men's Health Crisis (GMHC).

Even as GMHC, one of the largest AIDS service organizations in the USA, was coming into existence, members of Metropolitan Community Churches and Episcopal churches in New York, San Francisco and Los Angeles were voicing concern and taking action regarding AIDS and those infected by the virus. They thereby launched the very first religious community response to AIDS — a response "from the pews up". Those who had long worshipped together and shared church socials together were now together in the face of the virus as they had never been before. They began to provide personal care services including meals, house-cleaning, transportation to clinics or hospitals; they provided emergency financial assistance or housing; they offered free legal or dental services. And they began to devise new liturgical responses to their suffering.

From Kenneth South, AIDS National Interfaith Network,
Washington DC, USA

The celebration of life through renewal in worship

Worship — a special moment for celebration — attempts to place daily life on the stage. The repetition of gestures, words, sounds and colours that form the moment of celebration re-creates a reality that in many respects is also lived in an unconscious way.

More than the scheduled time of celebration, worship is the connection between this moment of celebration and life itself. It is a time for recognizing that we are created in God's image, a time to acknowledge our differences, to learn to be together, to be in touch, to overcome prejudices.

Worship calls the body in its totality to express moments of daily life and to recognize God's will and the importance of God's commitment to care for people and creation. Worship can help churches to remove the barriers we create in the everyday life of our human communities by opening up our eyes, our ears and all our senses to the extraordinary significance of "ordinary" experiences and to ways of expressing God's presence amidst the people and creation.

It is important to renew the ways in which we celebrate life and our faith as we worship together, as we read the Bible, pray and bring praise, and as we share experiences, life stories and bear one another's burdens. Some are challenged to enlarge their fellowship to include other Christian traditions and other faiths. In this fellowship the community joins hands and hearts for a service of healing for all humankind, amidst all the tragedies and all the suffering of our world; and it calls for the healing of people, cultures, nations and creation.

Worship services focusing on HIV/AIDS and those affected by it have been a vital element of the Strathclyde Interchurch AIDS Project in Scotland. People living with the virus and working on the front lines have been integrally involved in planning such services and developing creative ways of identifying and addressing the spiritual needs of those touched by HIV/AIDS. To begin with, these services were promoted primarily through the churches and through health board and social work outlets; later HIV/AIDS and gay and lesbian publications were used to inform those most likely to respond about the services. [1]

Safe places for sharing, telling and listening

The church can be a healing community only if it is truly a *sanctuary*, that is, a safe space, a healing space. For healing, people need a place where they can be comfortable in sharing their pain.

During a solidarity visit to Project Momentum, an AIDS project in the basement of a Roman Catholic Church in New York City, a woman pastor who co-ordinates the programme told about the experience of a woman who broke into tears when she participated in their meeting and openly shared, for the first time in her life, that she was living with HIV. It made her feel accepted and gave her a sense of wholeness and acceptance, as a whole person, in community.

From the report of a solidarity visit by the sub-group on pastoral care and healing community

The church needs to create an atmosphere of openness and acceptance. As noted earlier (p. 44), St Basil the Great taught that it is up to those in leadership positions in the church to create an environment, an ethos, a "disposition" for the cultivation of goodness and love in the community. The leadership of the church is called upon to nurture the seeds of the *Logos*, God's own word and God's own energy among the people. By creating a proper atmosphere or disposition, that "good moral action" which is love will issue forth in the lives of the human community.

Creating "safe spaces" for telling one's own story within our church communities is therefore a practical step through which congregations can become healing communities. The church, which is built upon and shaped around the master story of the gospels, can offer a forum where those who are afflicted can, in trust and acceptance, let down their guards and share their stories. Of course, this is not easily done. Self-disclosure, surrendering the chains of shame and guilt that have held one in bondage, may seem like a kind of "death". Many would rather keep the contents of such a story hidden — not realizing that a person's hold on the story is often as much the problem as the story's hold on the person.

Healing and care become more possible as one "shares the story" within an atmosphere of acceptance, love and continuing concern. The task for those in the ordained ministry of the church is to leave

---

The congregation of Trinity United Church of Christ in Chicago has a support ministry committee to deal with people living with HIV/AIDS. To become a member of the support ministry one must undergo 20 hours of training on HIV/AIDS and understand the United Church of Christ's theology of inclusiveness. The pastor is fully supportive of the ministry, which ensures confidentiality and a safe space for people in the church to share their stories. The church also offers other signs of accompaniment and solidarity for members to feel comfortable in sharing their pain and joy. Of the 7000 members, 5000 are wearing red ribbons in solidarity with people living with HIV/AIDS and those who have died.

Erlinda Senturias, from the report of a solidary visit to four cities in the USA

space in their own hearts and to allow their own egos to die, in order that this potential source of healing can flourish and bear fruit. This is the only way to create an atmosphere of acceptance in which stories can be shared. And this healing *needs* to happen among the people of the church.

The truth of the stories we share teaches us not only about others; it can also teach us about ourselves. Indeed, it is only in learning about ourselves that this healing is possible. People living with HIV/AIDS have shared many stories about themselves. They challenge us to change our understanding that "HIV = AIDS = death". They are living, they are struggling, they are teaching and learning — and they want all of us to enter into a new way of understanding life in community. People living with HIV/AIDS remind us that we are *all* vulnerable and in need of healing. We are challenged, therefore, to break the barriers between "us" and "them" because we *all* live with HIV/AIDS.

Weaving homes and community

The experience of AIDS highlights the shortcomings of traditional family and church structures. Many people are seeking other "spaces" for co-existence, self-discovery and self-affirmation. Leaving home and venturing into the unknown is a common experience among those living with HIV/AIDS.

The ethnographic survey carried out by the Institute of Religious Studies in Brazil in 1994 made it possible to interview and get to know a large number of people living with HIV/AIDS whose lives have been profoundly transformed by this new situation. They were re-thinking their lives, their relationships, their future, their destiny, the quality and intensity of their lives. People have sought, and in many cases found, a new home, a new family, perhaps provision-ally — but with the very deep-seated wish to recast family ties and relationships, with so many brothers and sisters discovered along the way. They have found a new home, rediscovered and rewritten with tears and dreams, as a "living space" for thousands of per-sons.

Ernesto Barros Cardoso

In Zaire a team visited a man who had been abandoned by his family because of his illness. He was pitifully lonely, waiting for visitors, and looking for what the team might be bringing for him. Some discussion began to build his confidence to take the initiative to call his family together. The team offered to come and talk with them in the hope of encouraging reconciliation. He invited them; and when the team left he was looking very different from when they first arrived. He was looking forward to an opportunity for family reconciliation, not just for his own benefit but for the well-being of his children and grandchildren all of whom, he felt, need to protect themselves.

Ian Campbell, in a report of a Salvation Army team visit to Zaire

However, many people living with HIV/AIDS are also returning to their homes, running the risk of admitting that they need to rebuild relationships and seeking reconciliation. In this way they can affirm that they are not "victims", but active participants in the restoration of the family and community.

Both individually and through informal groups which they have organized, people living with HIV/AIDS in Northern Thailand are becoming a force for redemption and healing in their local communities. Young widows whose husbands have died of AIDS cover stretches of dusty rural roads on motorbikes to sit with, hold the hand of, feed, bathe, caress and restore the hope of pain-wracked persons bereft of the will to live or to dream. Spontaneous support groups are appearing in homes and in roadside rest-spots where villagers, both HIV-infected and those not infected, share their experiences. All of these are vivid glimpses of the reality of true communion.

Thus it was, and has been for nearly two years now, that non-Christians in one part of Sankampang District have sought out the Christian pastor for comfort, support, solace and guidance, and have moved freely in and out of the church grounds, having come to see the church as a place of refuge, of release, of acceptance, of hope and of healing.

Prakai Nontawasee

The link between prevention and care

In living its identity as a caring community and in facilitating change, the church can develop practical approaches to HIV/AIDS. It is through caring with people that changes in attitudes, behaviours and the environment happen. This process of caring is linked to the response of people as they move towards their own change and healing. In so doing they help to prevent HIV/AIDS from spreading, and find hope for the future of their families and communities. They are living out the nature of true and loving care, which is to be *transforming*.

Caring can be expressed in various places where people can feel safe — at home, in the hospital, in drop-in centres — and it can be strengthened through the involvement of people from the whole community: neighbours, community leaders, church members, health professionals and those from various organizations. This involvement transforms people's lives — people living with HIV/AIDS, those intimately linked to them, the wider community and those doing the work. Care can provide an opportunity for exploring the meaning of creative and constructive change.

To help members of churches and communities understand the full dimension and impact of HIV/AIDS in their lives, participatory approaches are crucial. The AIDS pandemic should be regarded as a unique opportunity to revive and reinforce the values of responsibility, sexual integrity, healthy relationships, human dignity and mutual respect.

Focus group discussion in churches could be encouraged as a vital ministry. Questions such as the following could be raised: what does the church *uniquely* bring to efforts to face the challenges of HIV/AIDS? Has the church become a ghetto, isolated from the life of the people? Does the church touch people's existential lives? How can the church deal with, and be responsive to, the life of the community? How can the church be supported in identifying its priorities, and in tackling difficult issues related to its identity, life and mission? How can the church identify effective and relevant action to meet the challenge of HIV/AIDS? How can those in the church best reflect on what they have learned in meeting this challenge?

The role of the church should be seen in the light of its particular cultural context as well as in the light of the universal gospel message.

One church which has had the courage to engage in focus group discussion on HIV/AIDS is the Armenian Orthodox Church in Lebanon. The context of the life and mission of this church is the pluralistic society of Lebanon, in which this group of Lebanese Christians has maintained a particular way of life. Ideally, the church is where people seek solutions; but the church has in fact been shying away from the realities of everyday life. The church is slow in reacting to social issues. There is minimal dialogue with youth, and the church faces difficulties in preparing young people for sexuality. Religion and sexuality are not seen as contradictory, but finding practical approaches has been problematic. Moreover, many priests are poorly informed about HIV/AIDS. Their only source of information is what they read in newspapers or see on television. Action on HIV/AIDS is left to non-governmental organizations; it is not something the church is involved in. Therefore a need for priests to receive education on human sexuality is recognized.

This concrete experience from a parish in Lebanon is just one of many examples illustrating the need to equip churches with appropriate knowledge, skills and attitudes in meeting the challenge of HIV/AIDS.

People should develop a realistic understanding of vulnerability and risk, know the effectiveness of different preventive options and relate these to their own personal values. They should feel motivated to choose preventive behaviours, to practise relevant skills and to develop attitudes of compassion and care.

To promote the prevention of HIV-infection, frightening messages — using such images as skeletons, skulls, coffins and even open wounds — have often been transmitted in the hope of scaring people into behavioural change. Such messages are harmful. Not only do they suggest that unless one has such symptoms one is not infected, but they add to the stigma attached to those who are actually infected.

With HIV spreading everywhere, no preventive campaign can ignore that there are and will be more people infected and in need of support. The messages in a preventive campaign should therefore prepare people to take care of the infected and to show support for them. If we choose to use military language in this context and describe the virus as the "enemy", we must also make it very clear that the person carrying the virus is *not* the enemy, but a co-fighter against it.

Preventive work is indeed more effective when it engages persons who are living with HIV/AIDS. People listen and react when they hear the story of a person who is present before them, rather than merely seeing words on a page or drawings on a poster. Openness about HIV should be promoted, both to effect change and to extend support to those infected or affected.

Pastoral care and counselling

In practice AIDS counselling is often combined with health education, understood as teaching a client or patient how to behave and providing relevant information. But although information is an important dimension, counselling has other central aspects as well. Overall it should be seen as a helping or supporting process aimed at assisting persons in coping with their life-situation and accepting what has affected them.

Counselling is a process for *empowering* the person to make decisions about his or her own life. Beyond conveying information, the counselling process includes partnership in discussion and reflection about the specific problems and challenges the individual and his or her family are facing. In that sense, counselling may be concerned with many different areas of the life of a person or a family, and may address physical, practical, psychological, social and spiritual needs.

The goal of AIDS counselling in particular is twofold: to help infected persons come to terms with their situation; and to promote coping strategies for the infected and the affected, including preventing or reducing HIV-transmission.

Usually the arena for discussion, including any related testing and its associated counselling process, is one of confidentiality for the individual. Voluntary testing and counselling have been shown to be effective for support and prevention if a confidential environment is maintained.

While a variety of professionals may be involved in AIDS counselling, many professional counsellors would benefit from additional training in this specialized area. With proper training, concerned and dedicated volunteers may also be very good counsellors. Listening skills, the ability to empathize with persons in a vulnerable and difficult situation and the willingness to share the pain and grief in a counselling encounter are the main qualities which should be looked for when selecting potential counsellors.

A Guide to HIV/AIDS Pastoral Counselling, published by the World Council of Churches in 1990, is a practical manual with guidelines, information and case studies designed to help pastors and churches to improve their pastoral counselling skills.

A Journey of Love

Edward Dobson, the pastor of Calvary Church in Grand Rapids, Michigan, USA, and a member of the WCC Consultative Group on AIDS, said that difficulties arise for many evangelicals when care is extended to people outside the church who are living with HIV/AIDS. "Immediately tensions emerge: the tension of truth and love. How can we love people without legitimizing their choices? How can the church preach and model the ideal while at the same time confronting the reality?" But pursuing people in love can be an unpredictable journey. "I view this journey as an illustration of what happened when we decided to love some people who are ignored by many in the community. In the process of our journey we have learned some important lessons." Rev. Dobson shared one of his journeys:

"The envelope was not significantly different from the envelopes of the dozens of letters I get each week. But the contents would alter the direction of my life and ministry. It was a letter from a former member of our church. She had lost her husband, remarried and moved to another city. The letter was about her son Jim [not his real name]. Jim had grown up in our church. He attended Sunday school and was active in the youth group. But when he turned 18 he left the church for good. For many of his years in church he had struggled with his sexuality, and at 18 he left the Christian community and joined the gay community. When I received the letter, Jim was 35 and hospitalized in a serious condition. His mother feared that he had AIDS and asked if I would go and visit him.

"Jim was not the first person I knew with HIV/AIDS. There was Steve. I had travelled with Steve for an entire summer in an evangelistic team. Over the years I lost contact with him. Then someone told me he had died with complications from the virus (HIV/AIDS). There was Brian. Brian was a haemophiliac. I visited him many times. He also died of complications from the virus. The funeral director refused to open the casket at his funeral.

"It was a weekday evening when I went to the hospital to visit Jim. There was a sign on his door to check with the nursing station before entering his room. I did and was given the OK to go into the room. The room was dimly lit, and Jim was all alone. I introduced myself and told Jim that his mother had written me a letter and asked me to visit him. Jim did not say much.

"I told him that his mother feared he might have the virus. He told me that the doctor had just been in to see him, and his blood tests indicated he was HIV-positive. I was the first person he talked to since he got the news. I did not say a lot. I could tell he was afraid. I later found out that Jim thought he was going to die that night! I took his hand to offer a prayer. It was as if his hand was on fire. His fever was extremely high. After praying, I left him a copy of Billy Graham's book *Peace with God*.

"When I went to see him the next day his fever was broken and he was sitting up in bed. He had a smile on his face. 'I read the book,' he said, and 'I invited Christ into my life.' Soon Jim was released from the hospital and began a five-year war against the virus. We became friends. Jim occasionally attended our church. One of the families in our church 'adopted' him. They had him over to eat regularly and walked with him through his battle. He watched our television programme every week and often offered suggestions on how to improve it. We ate lunch together. We talked about the loneliness of his battle against HIV. We talked about his struggle with sexuality. We talked about the hatred and rejection of many Christians.

"The last time I was with him was again in a hospital room — the place where our friendship had begun. It was a few days before he died. AIDS had robbed his body of health, vitality and his eyesight. Two friends were with him. We joined hands together and prayed for Jim. I knew it would be my last prayer and it was hard to find words. Even as I write I am overcome with emotion."

Edward Dobson, in "HIV/AIDS: An Evangelical Perspective"

Community counselling

The counselling process which is applicable to an individual can also be applied to a group. This is done by building on the existing capacity to discuss issues of common concern.

Counselling as a community process can relate to both changes in attitude, behaviours and environments and to support. Skilled counselling can build inclusion, participation and capacity for agreement within the community.

In community counselling the presence of people living with HIV/AIDS is alluded to, but this is not connected specifically with those who are directly involved. These are kept in "shared confidentiality", meaning that people know the situation but do not discuss it directly. Instead, its meanings and implications are explored by the community members themselves. One major element of community confidentiality is "confidential sharing". If acknowledged, this can be a building block for facilitating a community response that links persons through their relationships to processes of support and change.

One example of this comes from Tshelanyemba, Zimbabwe, where community leaders came to understand the information about HIV/AIDS through interactive methods of education. Concerned, they began to meet together to discuss what they as leaders should do. Such spontaneous responses happen frequently when community leaders in any part of the world become aware; but this process can and should be facilitated so that it emerges more quickly and produces concrete action before the energy of commitment dissipates.

Knowing they had a resource in the AIDS team at the nearby hospital from which the educational resources had come, the Tshelanyemba leaders began to meed regularly with the team. At first there was an expectation that the hospital team would have "the answers"; but even when it became apparent that they did not, the commitment of everyone to the process was such that they could continue to facilitate joint exploration. This also taught the team something about the resourcefulness and determination of their community. The community became serious enough about the issues illuminated by HIV/AIDS to go on to tackle questions of alcohol use, migrant worker husbands, the drinking behaviour of men during the day, the sexual activity of their youth which was sometimes known to follow all-night prayer meetings, and the need to reflect on "codes of accountability", both those which already existed and those needed for future survival.

People of Christian faith are called to a service of reconciliation which links spiritual, biblical and theological themes to our response to HIV/AIDS in the areas of counselling and confidentiality. As an integral aspect of this response we must seek to capture the mystery of belonging, participation and mutual accountability — all of which are elements of confidentiality.

These elements, including the process of "confidential sharing", are realities existing in communities in different cultures. From them can develop an integrated care and prevention approach which accelerates a community's capacity to work together for positive change through respecting individual rights, while acknowledging community responsibility for both support and change. This is a source of hope and increased spiritual sensitivity for people and communities in the face of accumulated loss.

The HIV/AIDS pandemic challenges the church to rediscover and strengthen its ministry to those under threat of death or now dying. The church believes that hope is not lost when a person is infected with HIV; it believes that the spiritual resources of the church can be used to help people to accept, and to come to terms with, their own mortality. In all these concerns churches are well placed to work with local communities.

Case Study: The Strength of a Woman

The Church of Christ in Thailand has experienced the importance of community involvement in counselling and on this basis has developed case studies to assist churches in reflecting on pastoral care and healing community. These case studies, drawn from concrete experiences, include questions for discussion and reflection. One of these studies is as follows:

Arthit and Urai lived together with their six-year-old daughter Nut and Arthit's parents in a village about 30 km. south of Chiang Mai. They learned that they were both HIV-positive when they went for medical check-ups prior to deciding whether to have a second child. Arthit, angry with himself for having brought this upon his family, became suicidal. Urai's love, equanimity and firmness kept him from taking his life. "Whatever happens, we'll face it together," she said.

When Arthit was diagnosed with cryptococcal meningitis, he again felt discouraged and defeated. On top of the physical suffering came the pain inflicted by others. Neighbours stopped coming to visit for fear of contracting HIV. People in the market where Urai sold fresh vegetables avoided her stand, and her business slowed drastically. The family of Arthit's sister even took Nut away for fear that she would contract HIV by living under the same roof. Although he had been very close to his daughter, Arthit's own irrational fear even stopped him touching and holding Nut. He missed her comfort and warmth. He would not go outside the house, he stopped eating and he stopped taking care of himself. Still, Urai rose early each morning to go and sell her vegetables, only allowing herself to cry for a few minutes in the darkness before her husband awoke, refusing to let him see her tears. Again, it was her love, determination and commitment to him that made life worth fighting for and pulled Arthit back from despair.

After visiting a specialist at the hospital, and receiving medication for his meningitis, Arthit's condition improved within a matter of days.

Some time later Arthit and Urai heard about a Buddhist meditation centre where the abbot taught a technique designed for people living with AIDS. Based loosely on psychological and psychosomatic principles, and using a model which combined traditional Buddhist teachings and healing, it was providing many people with an effective spiritual discipline. It helped to release their pent-up emotions, focus their minds and clarify their thoughts and planning, resulting in improved health and a strengthened immune system. After a one-week session at the centre, they returned home feeling utterly renewed, refreshed, re-invigorated, and with new desire and energy for the struggle for life.

At home they kept up the meditation, growing stronger day by day. While pain, problems, obstacles, frustration, grief and family issues which brought disagreement and quarrels did not disappear, Urai and Arthit felt able to confront them one by one, day by day, without fear.

About this time they were introduced to the Church of Christ in Thailand's AIDS ministries team. The team visited weekly, brought basic medicine they needed and, more importantly, just sat and talked quietly with them, giving them a chance to express their feelings, giving voice to their thoughts and breath to their dreams. Soon Arthit's sister returned Nut to them, and Arthit himself packed away the thin mattress from the front room of the house where he had become accustomed to lying when he was sick or feverish. "I don't need it now," he said, "because there are no longer any sick people in this house." Urai gradually assumed the role of unofficial counsellor to people with problems in their district — anyone who needed a listening ear, a helping hand or a shoulder to cry on. She was a source of encouragement and hope for dozens of persons and families who were HIV-positive. Even some who had shunned her in the marketplace sought her help, asking what made her so strong in the midst of her crisis.

One day Urai appeared at the CCT AIDS ministries office with fear and confusion in her eyes. Arthit had terrible headaches, could not rise from bed, and there were new skin lesions even worse than before. "Does this mean he is really at the last stage now?", she whispered between gasps, with barely enough strength to force the words out. Then the tears, held back for months, came rushing out. We sat with her and let her cry until she finished, then found some pain medication for her to take to Arthit, and promised to visit them both the next day.

When members of the team arrived at their home, Arthit was just as Urai had described. Yet it became clear after only a few minutes of sitting and talking together that the most distressing and disheartening thing was that neither Arthit's father nor mother, nor anyone else in the household or neighbourhood dared to touch him. They were afraid even to spend more than a few moments at a time in the room with him. He wanted to sit and look out of the window, but no one would help him up. Our workers went to Arthit's side, touched his face and arms, and applied ointment to the affected skin. Placing their arms gently around his waist, they eased him to his feet, and supported him as he walked the few paces to the door to see the sunshine.

From that day nearly ten months ago, Arthit began to improve. He weighs more now than he did before getting sick, and while you might see the scars on his face and arms if you looked for them, you cannot help noticing the radiant smile which is on his face most of the time. It is a hard-won smile which comes from learning to live and love each day, one day at a time. Urai, still Arthit's rock, solace and joy, continues in good health offering friendship, advice, encouragement and hope to many others living with HIV. Some have formed an informal support group which meets regularly in their home. And reporting on what has been personal and family disaster, "I have found true love... I think it's worth it, don't you?"

Questions for discussion

1. In the context of the HIV/AIDS pandemic, how should Christians and churches respond to claims of healing potential (physical, spiritual and otherwise) arising from other traditions, such as Buddhist meditation or natural "folk" medicines?

2. Imagine yourself in Arthit's place. How would he feel about being touched, or physically cared for in the way he was by members of the CCT AIDS ministries team? How would you feel about being touched? How would feel if your parents refused to touch you?

3. In terms of mental, spiritual, social and relational health, how much of Arthit's and Urai's success in living with HIV/AIDS is due to medical care and treatment, and how much to other sources?

4. Consider Urai's role in this story. What observations, as general as they may be, would you venture to make regarding the role of women (wives, mothers, daughters, etc.) in Asian households during times of disease, death and crisis? Where does Urai's strength come from?

From a report by Prakai Nontawasee on the Church of Christ in Thailand's Health Promotion Unit; Source-Report on the Meeting of the Sub-Group on Pastoral Care and Healing Community, New York, pp.35-38

Support and counselling services, based in community life, should be encouraged by Christian communities. Christian pastoral care and counselling are complementary: pastoral care is a ministry of presence which each person can offer, while counselling is a process of helping people to make healthy choices for their lives. Christians working together in pastoral care and counselling can enable the sharing of burdens and of truth; they can be channels for reconciliation (cf. 2 Cor. 5:18). Drawing on the gifts of the Christian community, we can create teams of volunteers trained in pastoral care and counselling. As these gifts are offered, they can be more fully developed and used.

The needs of those who minister through giving pastoral care and counselling should also be remembered. Pastors and other care-givers need the time and opportunity to grieve for the deaths of those for whom they have cared. They need support in order to live creatively within the continuing stress of constant change and frequent loss.

NOTE

[1] Edith Campbell, "The Story of the Strathclyde Interchurch AIDS Project", in Michael S. Northcott, ed., *AIDS, Sex and the Scottish Churches*, Occasional Paper No. 29, Centre for Theology and Public Issues, University of Edinburgh, Edinburgh, 1993, pp.53f.

CHAPTER 7

Conclusion:
What the Churches Can Do

This study has made evident the delicate, interwoven relationships of human beings and their connectedness to all of life. It has proved neither desirable nor possible to do a one-dimensional study describing only the dramatic spread of AIDS and its devastating impact on those directly affected. Rather, the AIDS pandemic requires the analysis of a cluster of inter-related factors. These include the theological and ethical perspectives that inform, or arise from, our understanding of AIDS; the effects of poverty on individuals and communities; issues of justice and human rights; the understanding of human relationships; and the understanding of human sexuality. Of these the factor of sexuality has received the least attention within the ecumenical community; and further study in this area is essential for a deeper understanding of the challenges posed by HIV/AIDS.

Our exploration of these themes has brought us face to face with issues, understandings and attitudes which have major consequences for the churches in responding to the pandemic. Through their witness to the gospel of reconciliation, the value of each person and the importance of responsible life in community, the churches have a distinctive and crucial role to play in facing the challenges raised by HIV/AIDS. But if their witness is to be visible and active, it is essential to highlight the following concerns for common reflection and action:

A. The life of the churches: responses to the challenge of HIV/ AIDS

1. We ask the churches to provide a climate of love, acceptance and support for those who are vulnerable to, or affected by, HIV/

AIDS. This could be expressed by providing space for these concerns to be raised within regular worship, by special worship events (for example, in observance of World AIDS Day on 1 December), through support groups and by visits to those affected by HIV/AIDS.

2. We ask the churches to reflect together on the theological basis for their response to the challenges posed by HIV/AIDS.

3. We ask the churches to reflect together on the ethical issues raised by the pandemic, interpret them in their local context and offer guidance to those confronted by difficult choices.

4. We ask the churches to participate in the discussion in society at large of ethical issues posed by HIV/AIDS, and to support their own members who, as health care professionals, face difficult ethical choices in the areas of prevention and care.

B. The witness of the churches in relation to immediate effects and causes of HIV/AIDS

1. We ask the churches to work for better care for persons affected by HIV/AIDS.

2. We ask the churches to give particular attention to the conditions of infants and children affected by the HIV/AIDS pandemic and to seek ways to build a supportive environment.

3. We ask the churches to help safeguard the rights of persons affected by HIV/AIDS and to study, develop and promote the human rights of people living with HIV/AIDS through mechanisms at national and international levels.

4. We ask the churches to promote the sharing of accurate information about HIV/AIDS, to promote a climate of open discussion and to work against the spread of misinformation and fear.

5. We ask the churches to advocate increased spending by governments and medical facilities to find solutions to the problems — both medical and social — raised by the pandemic.

C. The witness of the churches in relation to long-term causes and factors encouraging the spread of HIV/AIDS

1. We ask the churches to recognize the linkage between AIDS and poverty, and to advocate measures to promote just and sustainable development.

2. We urge that special attention be focused on situations that increase vulnerability to AIDS such as migrant labour, mass refugee movements and commercial sex activity.

3. In particular, we ask the churches to work with women as they seek to attain the full measure of their dignity and express the full range of their gifts.

4. We ask the churches to educate and involve youth and men in order to prevent the spread of HIV/AIDS.

5. We ask the churches to seek to understand more fully the gift of human sexuality in the contexts of personal responsibility, relationships, family and Christian faith.

6. We ask the churches to address the pandemic of drug use and the role which this plays in the spread of HIV/AIDS and to develop locally relevant responses in terms of care, de-addiction, rehabilitation and prevention.

The Impact of HIV/AIDS and the Churches' Response

A statement adopted by the WCC central committee on the basis of the WCC consultative group on AIDS study process, September 1996

I. Introduction

1. Already in 1987 the executive committee of the World Council of Churches called the churches to address the urgent challenges posed by the spread of HIV/AIDS throughout the world. Appealing for an immediate and effective response in the areas of pastoral care, education for prevention and social ministry, the executive committee noted that "the AIDS crisis challenges us profoundly to be the church in deed and in truth: *to be the church as a healing community*".[1]

2. The spread of HIV infection and AIDS has continued at a relentless and frightening pace. The cumulative number of persons infected by the virus — women, men and children on all continents — is about 28 million by mid-1996; and it is estimated that 7000 new infections occur each day, including 1400 babies born infected. Individuals, communities, countries and churches are highly affected by this pandemic.

3. Given the tragic impact of AIDS on persons, communities and societies all over the world; given its direct impact upon many Christians and churches; recognizing the need for careful reflection on a number of inter-related issues bearing on the churches' understanding of and response to AIDS; and believing it imperative that the churches address *together* this issue of global concern, the WCC central committee at its meeting in Johannesburg in 1994 commissioned a comprehensive study to be done by a consultative group on AIDS.[2]

4. In its reflection the group has focused on theological and ethical issues raised by the HIV/AIDS pandemic, on questions of human rights in relation to AIDS, and on pastoral care and counselling within the church as a healing community. As it draws its findings into a final

report, the consultative group wishes to make available the present statement indicating some of the main concerns and implications of its work. We request that this statement be *adopted* by the central committee, that the report from the study be *welcomed* by central committee, and that both be shared with the churches for their reflection and appropriate action.

II. The impact of HIV/AIDS

5. HIV is a virus and, medically speaking, AIDS is the consequence of viral infection; but the issues raised by the pandemic are far from purely medical or clinical. They touch on cultural norms and practices, socio-economic conditions, issues of gender, economic development, human responsibility, sexuality and morality.

6. The HIV/AIDS pandemic is not just a matter of statistics. Its effects are impoverishing people, breaking their hearts, causing violations of their human rights and wreaking havoc upon their bodies and spirits. Many who suffer do so in rejection and isolation. In a striking way HIV/AIDS has become a "spotlight" revealing many iniquitous conditions in our personal and community lives, revealing our inhumanity to one another, our broken relationships and unjust structures. It reveals the tragic consequences of personal actions which directly harm others, or of negligence which opens people to additional risk. The pandemic exposes any silence and indifference of the churches, challenging them to be better informed, more active, and more faithful witnesses to the gospel of reconciliation in their own lives and in their communities.

7. Almost every day there are new discoveries, new information, new hopes and accounts of how communities are affected by, and are dealing with, the challenge of HIV/AIDS. The reality of the pandemic seems increasingly complex, confounding the generalizations, stereotypes and partial or false information which all too often dominate discussion of HIV/AIDS. We know, for example, that HIV/AIDS is not confined to particular groups within society, although in any given country particular groups may be more affected.

8. AIDS was first recognized in industrialized countries where, indeed, the vast majority of the funding for research, prevention and care has been concentrated. Now in its second decade, the pandemic is expanding fastest in countries with poor economies, where all the

economic, political and social mechanisms that keep countries poor interact to produce a context in which AIDS thrives. Thus AIDS has become a development issue. The HIV/AIDS pandemic adds a heavy burden on health-care systems. The cost of treatment is often completely disproportionate to the incomes of the affected families. In Thailand, for example, the cost of treatment for one person with AIDS absorbs up to 50 percent of an average annual household income.

9. AIDS impacts societies in many ways, challenging some traditional notions of the social order. In some places, the pandemic is raising questions about the meaning and role of the family; elsewhere it has focused attention on those using drugs and their increased risk; still elsewhere it has raised questions about human sexuality and relationships. In the course of the pandemic the role of gay communities in compassionate care and effective prevention has been recognized. This perspective has challenged the churches to rethink their relation to gay persons.

10. The pandemic is also having profound consequences for family and community life. In addition to causing the illness and death of members of the most productive age groups, it severely restricts the opportunities for those — for the most part, women and girls — who care for persons suffering from the disease. In some societies whole communities are weakened by the pain and disruption HIV/AIDS brings to families and other basic social units. Grandparents find themselves caring for their sick children or orphaned grandchildren, and children and young people are forced to become the breadwinners for others.

III. The beginnings of a response

11. The challenges posed by AIDS require both a global and a local response. How can we develop the will, knowledge, attitudes, values and skills required to prevent the spread of AIDS without the concerted efforts of governments, local communities, non-governmental organizations, research institutions, churches and other faith communities?

12. A full range of inter-related approaches is called for. Effective methods of prevention include sexual abstinence, mutual fidelity, condom use and safe practices in relation to blood and needles. Education, including education for responsible sexual practices, has

been shown to be effective in helping to stop the spread of the infection. Other measures which inhibit its spread or help to deal with the suffering which it causes include advocacy for justice and human rights, the empowerment of women, the training of counsellors and the creation of "safe spaces" where persons can share their stories and testimonies. In addition all societies — whether "developed" or developing — need to address practices such as drug abuse and commercial sex activity, including the increasing incidence of child prostitution, as well as the root causes of destructive social conditions such as poverty, all of which favour the spread of HIV/AIDS.

13. Strategies for prevention and care may fail if those affected by HIV/AIDS play no part in designing or carrying them out. In the course of the current study, the consultative group noted the role played by the WCC in promoting participatory action research on "AIDS and the Community as a Source of Care and Healing" in three African countries.[3] This process enabled village people to analyze the issues and problems raised by AIDS and to develop actions which foster prevention and care.

14. From the beginning of the pandemic some Christians, churches and church related institutions have been active in education and prevention programmes and in caring for people living with HIV/AIDS. The consultative group was privileged to have worked with several of these during the study. The group observes, however, that by and large the response of the churches has been inadequate and has, in some cases, even made the problem worse. As the WCC executive committee noted in 1987, "through their silence, many churches share responsibility for the fear that has swept our world more quickly than the virus itself".[4] Sometimes churches have hampered the spread of accurate information or created barriers to open discussion and understanding. Further, churches may reinforce racist attitudes if they neglect issues of HIV/AIDS because it occurs predominantly among certain ethnic or racial groups. These groups may be unjustly stigmatized as the most likely carriers of the infection.

15. The situation continues to call for "metanoia in faith" and a fresh resolve by the churches to address the situation directly. This must be done in a spirit of humility, knowing that we do not fully understand the scope and significance of the HIV/AIDS pandemic. It

requires openness to new information, long discussion of sensitive issues and readiness to learn from the experience of others, as we seek a more adequate response to the challenges posed by HIV/AIDS today.

IV. Theological dimensions

16. The HIV/AIDS pandemic raises difficult theological issues in the areas of creation, human nature, the nature of sin and death, the Christian hope for eternal life and the role of the church as body of Christ. Furthermore the reality of AIDS raises issues, such as human sexuality, vulnerability and mortality, which stir and challenge us in a deeply personal way. Christians and the churches struggle with these theological and human issues and they differ, sometimes sharply, in their response to some of the challenges posed by HIV/AIDS. But it is imperative that they learn to face the issues *together* rather than separately, and that they work towards a common understanding of the fundamental questions — theological, anthropological and ecclesiological — which are involved.

17. The church's response to the challenge of HIV/AIDS comes from its deepest theological convictions about the nature of creation, the unshakable fidelity of God's love, the nature of the body of Christ and the reality of Christian hope.

18. The creation in all its dimensions is held within the sphere of God's pervasive love, a love characterized by relationship, expressed in the vision of the Trinity as a model of intimate interaction, of mutual respect and of sharing without domination. This inclusive love characteristic of the Trinity guides our understanding of the Christian claim that men and women are made in the "image of God". Because humanity is created in God's image, all human beings are beloved by God and all are held within the scope of God's concern and faithful care.

19. Within the fullness of creation we affirm the potential for goodness of the human body and of human sexuality. We do not completely comprehend the meaning of human sexuality. As with other aspects of creation, sexuality also can be misused when people do not recognize their personal responsibility; but it is to be affirmed strongly as one of God's good gifts, finding expression in many dimensions of human existence. The churches have recognized mar-

riage as the primary place for the expression of sexuality in its various
dimensions.

20. We live from God's promise that nothing can separate us from
the love of God in Christ: no disasters, no illness or disease, nothing
done by us and nothing done to us, not even death itself, can break
God's solidarity with us and with all creation (Rom. 8.38-39). And yet
the creation "groans in travail" (Rom. 8:22); we see in the world much
suffering, injustice and waste. Some of this can be understood as the
consequence, for ourselves and others, of the exercise of the freedom
given by God to God's creatures; some of it, we sense, may be part of
a larger pattern of which we now glimpse only a part; some of it defies
understanding, leaving us to cry: "I believe; help my unbelief!" (Mark
9:24).

21. Finally we live by hope, holding our questions and doubts
within the larger frame of God's love and final purpose for our lives
and for all creation: life abundant, where justice reigns, where each is
free to explore all the gifts God has given them. More particularly, we
live by hope in Christ: Christ gone before us into glory is the basis for
our hope. We share in the sufferings of Christ — Christ who is
Immanuel, "God with us" — "that we may also be glorified with him"
(Rom. 8:17). And in our weakness we are sustained by the "Spirit who
lives within us", interceding when we know not how to pray and
finally granting anew "life to our mortal bodies" (Rom. 8:11,26; cf.
Eph. 3:16).

22. Strengthened by this hope, we wrestle with the profound
questions put to us by suffering. We affirm that suffering does not
come from God. We affirm that God is with us even in the midst of
sickness and suffering, working for healing and salvation even in "the
valley of the shadow of death" (Ps. 23:4). And we affirm that it is
through bearing the suffering of the world on the cross that God, in
Christ, has redeemed all of creation. Our hope is rooted ultimately in
our experience of God's saving acts in Jesus Christ, in Christ's life,
death and resurrection from the dead.

23. Remembering the suffering servant (Isa. 42:1-9; 49:1-7; 50:4-
11; 52:13-53:12), we are called to share the sufferings of persons
living with HIV/AIDS, opening ourselves in this encounter to our own
vulnerability and mortality. This is to walk with Christ; and as Christ
has gone before us through death to glory, we are called to receive

"the sure and certain hope of the resurrection". This is God's promise that God's promise, for us and for all creation, is not destroyed by death: we are held within the love of God, claimed by Christ as his own and sustained by the Spirit; and God will neither forsake us nor leave us to oblivion.

24. We affirm that the church as the body of Christ is to be the place where God's healing love is experienced and shown forth. As the body of Christ the church is bound to enter into the suffering of others, to stand with them against all rejection and despair. Because it is the body of *Christ* — who died for all and who enters into the suffering of all humanity — the church cannot exclude anyone who needs Christ. As the church enters into solidarity with those affected by HIV/AIDS, our hope in God's promise comes alive and becomes visible to the world.

25. We celebrate the commitment of many Christians and churches to show Christ's love to those affected by HIV/AIDS. We confess that Christians and churches have also helped to stigmatize and discriminate against persons affected by HIV/AIDS, thus adding to their suffering. We recall with gratitude the advice of St Basil the Great to those in leadership positions within the church, emphasizing their responsibility to create an environment — an ethos, a "disposition" — where the cultivation of love and goodness can prevail within the community and issue in the "good moral action" which is love.[5]

26. We affirm that God calls us to live in right relationship with other human beings and with all of creation. As a reflection of God's embracing love, this relationship should be marked not just by mutual respect but by active concern for the other. Actions taken deliberately which harm oneself, others or the creation are sinful; and indeed we are challenged by the persistence of sin, which is the distortion of this right relationship with God, other persons, or the natural order. Yet sin does not have the last word; as we are "renewed by the Holy Spirit" (cf. Titus 3:5) and continue to grow in our communion with God, our lives will show forth more of God's love and care.

27. The World Council of Churches executive committee emphasized in a 1987 statement the need "to affirm that God deals with us in love and mercy and that we are therefore freed from

simplistic moralizing about those who are attacked by the virus".[6] Furthermore we note how easily a moralistic approach can distort life within the Christian community, hampering the sharing of information and open discussion which are so important in facing the reality of HIV/AIDS and in inhibiting its spread.

28. In the light of these reflections, and on the basis of our experience in this study, we wish to avoid any implication that HIV/AIDS, or indeed any disease or misfortune, is a direct "punishment" from God. We affirm that the response of Christians and the churches to those affected by HIV/AIDS should be one of love and solidarity, expressed both in care and support for those touched directly by the disease, and in efforts to prevent its spread.

V. Ethical dimensions

29. In responding to the challenge of HIV/AIDS Christians are motivated by urgent imperatives, passionately felt: to show Christ's love for the neighbour, to save lives, to work for reconciliation, to see that justice is done. Making ethical decisions, however, requires a process of *discernment* which includes gathering the latest information, wrestling with deeply sensitive issues and weighing differing, sometimes conflicting views and interests. This process needs to be undergirded by Bible study, prayer and theological reflection.

30. Christians make ethical choices following principles which derive from their understanding of the biblical witness and their faith convictions. These may be stated and developed differently in various traditions, but are likely to include the following points:

* because all human beings are created and beloved by God, Christians are called to treat every person as of infinite value;
* because Christ died to reconcile all to God, Christians are called to work for true reconciliation — which includes justice — among those alienated from one another;
* because we are "members one of another", being built up by the Spirit into one body, Christians are called to responsible life within community.

31. Such principles — the infinite value of each person, the gospel of reconciliation, the call to responsible life within community — have to be applied to such questions as: How do churches respond to their members living with HIV/AIDS? How can churches promote

responsible behaviour without being judgmental and moralistic? What public health measures to reduce HIV/AIDS transmission should churches advocate? How can resources for care and research be fairly shared? This means in each case exploring all available options, weighing the benefits (and difficulties) of each, and finally asking, "which of the possible courses of action best expresses Christ's love for all those involved?"

32. Such a process of discernment is often difficult: the options may not be fully clear; none of the options may be wholly satisfactory; the implications of some biblical or theological principles for specific problems today may not be clear. It is all the more important, then, that Christians and churches reflect and work on these ethical issues *together*. The challenge of HIV/AIDS demands nothing less than an *ecumenical* response.

33. Churches are expected to give both spiritual direction and moral guidance, and to play a responsible role in the discussion of these issues in the wider society, as well as in discussions of biomedical ethics. Witnessing to their own faith convictions, they enrich the wider debate and make common cause, where possible, with persons of goodwill who appeal to more general sets of ethical principles such as respect for persons, beneficence and non-maleficence, and justice.

34. The churches have crucial contributions to make to this wider debate. For example first, in accordance with their *commitment to truth* they can emphasize that the process of ethical discernment leaves no room for judgments based on superficial generalizations or stereotypes, on fear, or on incomplete or false information. The churches can do much to promote, both in their own lives and in the wider society, a climate of sensitive, factual and open exploration of the ethical issues posed by the pandemic.

35. Second, in accordance with their *emphasis upon personal and communal responsibility* the churches can promote conditions — personal, cultural, and socio-economic — which support persons in making responsible choices. This requires a degree of personal freedom which is not always available: for example, women, even within marriage, may not have the power to say "no" or to insist on the practice of such effective preventive measures such as abstinence, mutual fidelity and condom use.

VI. Human rights in relation to HIV/AIDS

36. The HIV/AIDS pandemic raises important issues relating to human rights. People living with HIV/AIDS generally encounter fear, rejection and discrimination, and often are denied basic rights (such as liberty, autonomy, security and freedom of movement) enjoyed by the rest of the population. Because such reactions contradict the values of the gospel, the churches are called to formulate and advocate a clear policy of non-discrimination against persons living with HIV/AIDS.

37. One of the tasks of the WCC over the last three decades has been to be actively involved in human rights standard setting, promotion and protection. The last decade has witnessed a significant trend in the development of international norms and standards in relation to people that are discriminated against on grounds of race, gender, ethnicity and religion. There are other kinds of discrimination as well. Some of them arise because of lack of awareness and fear. People living with HIV/AIDS fall in this category. They are often denied their fundamental right to security, freedom of association, movement and adequate health care.

38. The issue of human rights also has important implications for the spread of HIV/AIDS. We note the alarming rise in sex tourism. Some men in societies in both the North and the South abuse the young and poor children for prostitution or in an effort to try to escape infection. This is also an issue of violence against children. We further note that men and women who are denied their fundamental human rights, whether on the grounds of social status, sexual orientation or addiction to drugs, are thereby made especially vulnerable to the risk of HIV infection. Thus broadly-based strategies which advocate human rights are required to prevent the spread of HIV.

VII. Pastoral care and counselling within the church as healing community

39. By their very nature as communities of faith in Christ, churches are called to be healing communities. This call becomes the more insistent as the AIDS pandemic continues to grow. Within the churches we are increasingly confronted with persons affected by HIV/AIDS, seeking support and solidarity and asking: are you willing to be my brother and sister within the one body of Christ? In this encounter our very credibility is at stake.

40. Many churches, indeed, have found that their own lives have been enhanced by the witness of persons living with HIV/AIDS. These have reminded us that it is possible to affirm life even when faced with severe, incurable illness and serious physical limitation, that sickness and death are not the standard by which life is measured, that it is the quality of life — whatever its length — that is most important. Such a witness invites the churches to respond with love and faithful caring.

41. Despite the extent and complexity of the problems, the churches can make an effective healing witness towards those affected by HIV/AIDS. The experience of love, acceptance and support within a community where God's love is made manifest can be a powerful healing force. Healing is fostered where churches relate to daily life and where people feel safe to share their stories and testimonies. Through sensitive worship, churches help persons enter the healing presence of God. The churches exercise a vital ministry through encouraging discussion and analysis of information, helping to identify problems and supporting participation towards constructive change in the community.

42. Many trained and gifted members of the community, as well as some pastors, are already providing valuable pastoral care. Such care includes counselling as a process for empowerment of persons affected by HIV/AIDS, in order to help them deal with their situation and to prevent or reduce HIV transmission.

VIII. Conclusion: what the churches can do

43. This study has shown us the delicate, interwoven relationships of human beings and their connectedness to all of life. It has proved neither desirable nor possible to do a "one-dimensional" study of AIDS, describing only its dramatic spread and devastating impact on those who are directly affected. Rather, the AIDS pandemic requires the analysis of a cluster of inter-related factors. These include the theological and ethical perspectives that inform, or arise from, our understanding of AIDS; the effects of poverty on individuals and communities; issues of justice and human rights; the understanding of human relationships; and the understanding of human sexuality. Of these the factor of sexuality has received the least attention within the ecumenical community. We recognize that further study in this area is

essential for a deeper understanding of the challenges posed by HIV/AIDS.

44. Our exploration of these themes has brought us face to face with issues, understandings and attitudes of major consequence to the churches and their role in responding to the pandemic. Through their witness to the gospel of reconciliation, the value of each person, and the importance of responsible life in community, the churches have a distinctive and crucial role to play in facing the challenges raised by HIV/AIDS. But their witness must be visible and active. Therefore we feel it essential to highlight the following concerns as points for common reflection and action by the churches:

A. The life of the churches: responses to the challenge of HIV/AIDS

1. We ask the churches to provide a climate of love, acceptance and support for those who are vulnerable to, or affected by, HIV/AIDS.

2. We ask the churches to reflect together on the theological basis for their response to the challenges posed by HIV/AIDS.

3. We ask the churches to reflect together on the ethical issues raised by the pandemic, interpret them in their local context and to offer guidance to those confronted by difficult choices.

4. We ask the churches to participate in the discussion in society at large of ethical issues posed by HIV/AIDS, and to support their own members who, as health care professionals, face difficult ethical choices in the areas of prevention and care.

B. The witness of the churches in relation to immediate effects and causes of HIV/AIDS

1. We ask the churches to work for better care for persons affected by HIV/AIDS.

2. We ask the churches to give particular attention to the conditions of infants and children affected by the HIV/AIDS pandemic and to seek ways to build a supportive environment.

3. We ask the churches to help safeguard the rights of persons affected by HIV/AIDS and to study, develop and promote the human rights of people living with HIV/AIDS through mechanisms at national and international levels.

4. We ask the churches to promote the sharing of accurate information about HIV/AIDS, to promote a climate of open discussion and to work against the spread of misinformation and fear.

5. We ask the churches to advocate increased spending by governments and medical facilities to find solutions to the problems — both medical and social — raised by the pandemic.

C. The witness of the churches: in relation to long-term causes and factors encouraging the spread of HIV/AIDS

1. We ask the churches to recognize the linkage between AIDS and poverty, and to advocate measures to promote just and sustainable development.

2. We urge that special attention be focussed on situations that increase the vulnerability to AIDS such as migrant labour, mass refugee movements and commercial sex activity.

3. In particular, we ask the churches to work with women as they seek to attain the full measure of their dignity and express the full range of their gifts.

4. We ask the churches to educate and involve youth and men in order to prevent the spread of HIV/AIDS.

5. We ask the churches to seek to understand more fully the gift of human sexuality in the contexts of personal responsibility, relationships, family and Christian faith.

6. We ask the churches to address the pandemic of drug use and the role this plays in the spread of HIV/AIDS and to develop locally relevant responses in terms of care, de-addiction, rehabilitation and prevention.

NOTES

[1] Quoted in the *Minutes* of the 38th meeting of the WCC central committee, Geneva, WCC, 1987, Appendix VI, "AIDS and the Church as a Healing Community", p.133.

[2] *Minutes* of the 45th meeting of the WCC central committee, Geneva, WCC, 1994, pp.45-49, 102f.

[3] See *Participatory Action Research on AIDS and the Community as a Source of Care and Healing*, Geneva, Christian Medical Board of Tanzania, Uganda Protestant Medical Bureau, Eglise du Christ au Zaire and WCC, 1993.

[4] *Loc. cit.*, p.135.

[5] *Ascetic Works*, 2.1.

[6] *Loc. cit.*, p.135.

An HIV/AIDS Glossary

Affected: a term used for the family, friends and other persons associated with someone living with HIV/AIDS.

AIDS (*Acquired Immune Deficiency Syndrome*): a group of signs and symptoms or a combination of diseases caused by the Human Immunodeficiency Virus (HIV), which impairs the body's ability to fight infection, making it especially susceptible to opportunistic infections, of which the most common include pneumocystis carinii pneumonia and certain cancers, such as Kaposi's sarcoma, a skin cancer.

AIDS test: a misnomer sometimes incorrectly used to refer to the HIV antibody test.

Focus group discussion: a method for group analysis and problem-solving, stressing the role of the group in identifying its own problems, and seeking transformative solutions appropriate to the local situation (see participatory action research, below).

HIV (*Human Immunodeficiency Virus*): the virus that can eventually cause AIDS. People infected with HIV may look and feel well for a number of years before any opportunistic infections develop. Many people infected with the HIV virus are completely unaware of the fact, unless they decide to have a medical blood test. However, they can be carriers of the virus, transmitting it to other people.

HIV antibody test: a laboratory test made on a small sample of blood to detect whether the body has reacted to the presence of HIV by trying to protect itself against the virus through producing antibodies. Though the presence of antibodies indicates that a person has been exposed to the virus, their absence does not necessarily mean that the person is not infected with HIV, since this reaction takes an average of three months after infection to show up in the blood. If the test is positive, the infected person will have been able to pass on the virus from the moment of infection. It is not possible to tell from this test when or how the person tested will proceed to AIDS.

HIV-positive (or *seropositive*): a term indicating that the HIV antibody test on a person has indicated the presence of antibodies in the blood. If the test is positive, it means that the person has been exposed to HIV and that his or her immune system has developed antibodies to the virus.

Immune deficiency: impairment of the body's ability to resist infection.

Immune system: the body's natural defence system which protects it from infection by recognizing bacteria, viruses and diseases in general. It consists of cells that (among other things) produce antibodies, which can recognize materials as foreign to the body and then attempt to neutralize them without injury to the person's cells.

Incubation period: the period of time between infection by the disease-causing organism and the onset of signs and symptoms of the disease. In people with HIV infection, the average incubation period is seven to ten years.

Infected: a term used for a person who has the HIV virus within his or her body.

IVDU (*Intravenous Drug Use*): one of four main high-risk behavioural patterns resulting in HIV infection. Drug use may involve using and often sharing unsterilized needles and syringes that serve to transmit HIV.

Opportunistic infection: an infection caused by an otherwise harmless micro-organism that can become pathogenic when the host's resistance is impaired.

Participatory action research: a process of community-building and empowerment for identifying, analyzing and solving problems at the community level. This approach seeks practical, locally-appropriate (rather than abstract or "universal") solutions, and uses such methodologies as key informant interviews, close local observation, survey questionnaires, rapid appraisal, and focus group discussion (see above).

Transmission: the spread of the disease-causing organism from one person to another. The major modes of transmission of HIV are penetrative sexual intercourse, shared contaminated equipment of intravenous drug users, transfusion of unscreened blood (blood which has not been tested) and from mother to unborn or newborn infant.

TERMS TO AVOID

Terms to avoid	Why to avoid them	Use instead
Carrying AIDS, AIDS carrier, AIDS positive	These terms confuse two distinct phases: being infected with HIV and having AIDS. People can have AIDS, but they cannot "carry" it.	HIV-antibody positive; people with HIV.
AIDS test	The most commonly used test detects antibodies to HIV. There cannot be a test for AIDS; the diagnosis for AIDS is based on clinical symptoms.	HIV antibody test.
AIDS virus	This term can lead to confusion between HIV and AIDS.	HIV (Human Immuno-deficiency Virus).
Catch AIDS	It is not possible to "catch" AIDS. Although it is possible to "catch" HIV, this is a misleading expression, because it may suggest that transmission of HIV is similar to transmission of colds or flu.	Contract HIV; become infected with HIV; become HIV- positive.
AIDS sufferer	Having AIDS does not mean being sick all the time. Someone with AIDS can continue to work and lead a normal life for some time after diagnosis. The term "suffering"is thus inappropriate.	Person with AIDS.

Terms to avoid	Why to avoid them	Use instead
AIDS victim	The language of "victim" suggests helplessness.	Person with AIDS, person who has AIDS.
Innocent victim	This term implies that anyone else with AIDS is "guilty".	
High-risk groups	The fact of being classified as a member of any particular group does not put anyone at greater risk; it is what he or she does, regardless of group, that may put him or her at greater risk. In other words, one should speak of risk behaviour, not of high risk groups.	High-risk be-haviour.

This material has been adapted from Beverly Booth, "Health Professionals and the AIDS Epidemic: Say What You Mean and Mean What You Say", *Contact*, no. 136, Apr. 1994, pp.10f.; and *Guide to HIV/AIDS Pastoral Counselling*, Geneva, WCC AIDS Working Group, 1990, pp.v-vii.

Persons Involved in the HIV/AIDS Study Process

MEMBERS OF THE WCC CONSULTATIVE GROUP

Prof. Joseph Allen was formerly professor at Holy Cross Greek Orthodox School of Theology, Brookline, Massachusetts, and at St Vladimir's Orthodox Seminary, Crestwood, New York. He is currently director of the Antiochian House of Studies within the Antiochian Orthodox Christian Archdiocese of North America. His paper, "The Christian Understanding of Human Relations: Resource for the Churches' Response to AIDS" was published in *The Ecumenical Review*, Vol. 47, no. 3, July 1995, pp.353ff.

Dr Christoph Benn (moderator) was formerly AIDS Coordinator of the German Institute for Medical Missions in Tübingen, Germany. He is currently a physician in the Paul Lechler Tropenheim Klinik in Tübingen, Germany. He has received training in both medicine and theology.

Hierdeacon Anatoly Berestov is a pediatrician and neurologist and an hierdeacon in the Russian Orthodox Church. He was a member of the sub-group on theology and ethics.

Mr Joao Guilherme Biehl is a Brazilian lay theologian and social anthropologist. He was one of the editors of *Making Connections: Facing AIDS* — an HIV resource book published by the youth desk of the World Council of Churches. He is presently teaching anthropology at the Federal University in Salvador, Bahia, Brazil.

Ms Mary Susan Caesar is a lawyer from South Africa and active in the youth programme of the Western Province Council of Churches in South Africa. She was a member of the sub-group on human rights.

Capt. (Dr) Ian Campbell is the International Health Programme consultant of the Salvation Army, based in London and Australia. He worked in Chikankata Hospital, Zambia, in the 1980s and developed the concept of an integrated response to HIV and AIDS as an opportunity for community development and change. He has served as consultant to UNAIDS meetings.

Mr Ernesto Cardoso (deceased) was a Brazilian Methodist lay theologian, musician, composer, and animator for groups and events. He coordinated the Latin American Council of Churches (CLAI) Liturgy Network and worked with the Institute for Religious Studies (ISER) as a coordinator of the "Gestures, Colours and Sound: Liturgical Renewal and Spirituality in Latin America" project. He was diagnosed HIV-positive in 1990 and died on 20 December 1995.

Rev. Edward Dobson is an evangelical pastor of the Calvary Church in Grand Rapids, Michigan, USA. He was a member of the sub-group on pastoral care and healing community. He is actively engaged in AIDS ministry.

Prof. Dr T. Jacob John, a lay member of the Malankara Syrian Orthodox Church, is an emeritus medical scientist (Indian Council of Medical Research). He was formerly head of the Department of Microbiology and Virology of the Christian Medical College in Vellore. He is a pediatrician and virologist. His paper "Sexuality, Sin and Disease: Theological and Ethical Issues Posed by AIDS to the Churches" was published in *The Ecumenical Review*, Vol. 47, no. 3, July 1995, pp.373ff.

Mr Simon Moglia is a member of the Uniting Church of Australia. He worked with the youth department of the National Council of Churches in Australia and is a member of the general committee of the Christian Conference of Asia. He has studied theology and is presently a law student.

Rev. Dr Prakai Nontawasee is a member of the WCC central committee. She holds several leadership positions in the Church of Christ in Thailand, and is a former president of the Christian Conference of Asia. She is a member of the McGilvaray Faculty of Theology, Chiang Mai, Thailand.

Rev. Dr Ruth Page is a member of the WCC central committee and of the commission on Programme Unit II. A theologian and member of the Church of Scotland, she is now principal of New College, Edinburgh.

Ms Haydee Pellegrini is an economist and a Roman Catholic lay theologian. She is in the leadership of the Global Network of People Living with HIV/AIDS and has spoken and lobbied in various international conferences on HIV/AIDS. She is from Uruguay but now lives in Argentina.

Dr Bulisi Pongo is a member of the commission on Programme Unit II of the WCC. He is the director general of the Kimbanguist medical department of the Church of Jesus Christ on Earth in Kinshasa, Zaire.

The Rev. Erin Shoemaker is an ordained minister of the United Church of Christ in Canada. She is actively engaged in the AIDS ministry and in working with lesbian and gay communities.

Ms Anne Skjelmerud is a member of the Lutheran Church in Norway. She works with the Centre for Partnership in Development in Oslo and is a consultant to Norwegian Church Aid.

Mrs Sri Winarti Soedjatmoko is a member of the WCC central committee and a member of the East Java Christian Church (Indonesia). She participated in the New Delhi meeting as a substitute for Prakai Nontawasee.

Dr Jihane Tawilah is a Maronite who works with the World Health Organization office in Lebanon and in the National AIDS Programme. She has assisted the Middle East Council of Churches in its ministry on AIDS and addiction.

Rev. Laisiasa Wainikesa is a member of the Methodist Church in Fiji. He is an AIDS educator in the Pacific region and has been a consultant for the World Health Organization and UNESCO in the Pacific region.

Rev. Neilson Waithe is an ordained minister of the Moravian Church in the Eastern Caribbean. He currently serves as vice chairperson of the province and superintendent of the Moravian Church in his native

Barbados. He pastors two churches and is actively engaged in counselling. He has written the book *Caribbean Sexuality.*

Rev. Flora Winfield is an Anglican priest and chaplain of Mansfield College, Oxford, England. Her paper "For Nothing Can Separate Us from the Love of Christ – Who *Does* Belong to the Body of Christ?" was published in *The Ecumenical Review*, Vol. 47, no. 3, July 1995, pp. 364ff.

Dr Rose Zoé-Obianga is professor of French linguistics at the University of Cameroon. From the Presbyterian Church of Cameroon, she has been a member of the executive group of the Unit II commission of WCC and a vice-president of the All Africa Conference of Churches.

KEY RESOURCE PERSONS

Rev. Dr Kenneth Boyd is an ethicist and professor at the Institute of Medical Ethics, Department of Medicine, Edinburgh University.

Ms Julia Hausermann is a barrister-at-law and human rights expert. She is the executive chair of Rights and Humanity, based in London.

Dr Joop Groen is a member of the Reformed Church in the Netherlands and presently acting director of Rainbow Foundation in Amsterdam.

Rev. Kenneth South is executive director, AIDS National Interfaith Network, Washington DC, USA.

WCC STAFF MEMBERS

Rev. Samuel Ada
Rev. Dr Thomas Best
Sr Monica Cooney, smsm
Mr Mark Halton
Mr Jan Kok
Mr Clement John
Ms Lee Ye Ja
Dr Salwa Morcos

Ms Jenny Roske
Dr Gert Rüppell
Rev. Dr Ioan Sauca
Ms Anu Talvivaara
Ms Odile Thiers
Dr Erlinda N. Senturias
Mr Marlin VanElderen

RUSSIAN INTERPRETER

Ms Zinaida Nossova